Wordly Wise

Kenneth Hodkinson

BOOK 8
Revised

Educators Publishing Service, Inc.
Cambridge and Toronto

Cover Design/ Hugh Price

Educators Publishing Service, Inc.
31 Smith Place, Cambridge, MA 02138

May 2000 Printing

Contents

WORD LIST v

INTRODUCTION ix

CHAPTER ONE
    Word List — Lesson 1 1
    Word List — Lesson 2 4
    Word List — Lesson 3 8
    Chapter One Crossword Puzzle 13

CHAPTER TWO
    Word List — Lesson 4 14
    Word List — Lesson 5 16
    Word List — Lesson 6 20
    Chapter Two Crossword Puzzle 25

CHAPTER THREE
    Word List — Lesson 7 26
    Word List — Lesson 8 28
    Word List — Lesson 9 32
    Chapter Three Crossword Puzzle 37

CHAPTER FOUR
    Word List — Lesson 10 38
    Word List — Lesson 11 41
    Word List — Lesson 12 44
    Chapter Four Crossword Puzzle 49

CHAPTER FIVE
    Word List — Lesson 13 50
    Word List — Lesson 14 53
    Word List — Lesson 15 56
    Chapter Five Crossword Puzzle 61

CHAPTER SIX
    Word List — Lesson 16 62
    Word List — Lesson 17 65
    Word List — Lesson 18 68
    Chapter Six Crossword Puzzle 73

CHAPTER SEVEN
    Word List — Lesson 19 74
    Word List — Lesson 20 77
    Word List — Lesson 21 81
    Chapter Seven Crossword Puzzle 85

CHAPTER EIGHT

Word List – Lesson 22 86

Word List – Lesson 23 89

Word List – Lesson 24 92

Chapter Eight Crossword Puzzle 97

CHAPTER NINE

Word List – Lesson 25 98

Word List – Lesson 26 101

Word List – Lesson 27 105

Chapter Nine Crossword Puzzle 109

CHAPTER TEN

Word List – Lesson 28 110

Word List – Lesson 29 113

Word List – Lesson 30 116

Chapter Ten Crossword Puzzle 121

Word List

(Numbers in parentheses refer to the Word List in which the word appears)

ABATTOIR (22)
abortive (4)
abstruse (23)
abut (22)
accolade (5)
accouter (10)
accrue (19)
acetic (1)
acolyte (13)
acronym (24)
affinity (11)
agenda (6)
aggregate (28)
aggrieved (22)
ague (14)
ambulatory (7)
amity (29)
amorphous (20)
analgesic (25)
animalcule (2)
anoint (15)
anomalous (4)
antediluvian (26)
anterior (16)
antipathy (5)
antiquary (23)
apoplectic (6)
apothecary (8)
archetype (24)
argosy (27)
asperity (12)
aspersion (22)
asphyxiate (3)
asseverate (17)
atavism (13)
attrition (25)
auspices (23)
autocrat (30)
avouch (26)
axiom (10)

BACCHANALIAN (11)
banal (14)
bandanna (12)

baneful (15)
beatific (18)
bedizen (13)
bereft (10)
biennial (21)
blandishment (16)
blasphemous (11)
boon (14)
brevity (19)
brier (15)
bromide (20)

CADENCE (24)
canto (13)
captious (4)
carapace (17)
cardiac (22)
carmine (5)
catholic (9)
caucus (21)
celerity (19)
celibate (20)
centaur (27)
cerebral (25)
chauvinist (26)
circumspect (6)
circumvent (7)
clairvoyant (14)
clandestine (1)
claustrophobia (18)
clement (28)
climacteric (16)
clique (17)
coadjutor (4)
coalesce (5)
cognate (15)
cohort (29)
collateral (2)
colloquial (8)
commiserate (30)
compliant (27)
composite (21)
composure (19)
conclave (12)

concomitant (18)
congeal (28)
congruence (23)
conjugal (16)
connubial (17)
consanguinity (20)
consummate (24)
contiguous (21)
contingent (29)
contumely (25)
cornucopia (3)
corollary (18)
correlate (9)
cortege (10)
cosmic (1)
coterie (19)
crevice (13)
crustacean (20)
cuckold (7)
curate (8)
cyst (14)

DEBAUCHED (26)
decant (22)
decennial (11)
deduce (9)
deem (15)
defeatist (30)
defect (28)
defray (2)
deify (13)
deliquesce (27)
demagogue (14)
demulcent (25)
denude (6)
depose (12)
depredation (16)
desecrate (29)
desist (3)
devolve (1)
dewlap (23)
diadem (24)
diaphanous (21)
dichotomy (22)

didactic (7)
dipsomaniac (15)
disconsolate (2)
disdain (10)
dishabille (23)
disjointed (4)
disquisition (30)
dissect (19)
dissemble (8)
disseminate (28)
dissimulate (5)
dissonance (26)
distrait (29)
doctrine (17)
dolorous (18)
dote (6)
dross (27)
ductile (13)
durance (9)

ECOLOGY (25)
educe (4)
effeminate (3)
effete (1)
efficacy (30)
effigy (26)
effrontery (7)
egoism (14)
egotism (5)
elide (27)
embrasure (20)
emeritus (2)
emissary (15)
emote (6)
empathy (3)
empirical (4)
empyrean (16)
enclave (25)
endemic (26)
ennobling (13)
enrapture (28)
ensemble (1)
entity (27)
epicure (29)

epidemic (17)
epidermis (21)
epilogue (8)
epitome (25)
equable (2)
equivocal (9)
ersatz (18)
erupt (5)
ethereal (7)
evanescent (3)
eviscerate (8)
exacerbate (6)
excerpt (30)
excrescence (9)
exculpate (4)
exhume (1)
exigencies (7)
exiguous (14)
exorcise (8)
expatiate (11)
expiate (16)
extradite (15)

FAKIR (26)
fatalism (19)
febrile (28)
felicitous (5)
fey (6)
fiord (20)
firmament (4)
flotsam (13)
foment (2)
frangible (22)
friable (29)
frieze (3)
fructify (21)
fulgent (19)
fumigate (20)
fuselage (12)
fusillade (1)
fustian (21)

GARGOYLE (7)
gelid (19)

v

genealogy (8)
generate (20)
gentility (27)
gentry (21)
ghetto (23)
gloaming (14)
gossamer (15)
grandiose (25)
gratuitous (10)
gubernatorial (13)

HABILIMENTS (26)
halcyon (9)
hansom (30)
hedonism (28)
heritage (27)
hibernate (29)
hirsute (7)
homogeneous (11)

IDIOSYNCRASY (30)
imbecile (19)
imbroglio (24)
imbue (22)
impeach (2)
impecunious (8)
importune (20)
impropriety (14)
inalienable (25)
inanimate (9)
incantation (7)
incarnate (28)
incommunicado (15)
indite (3)
infiltrate (30)
inflect (5)
influx (12)
infraction (1)
ingenue (21)
ingot (29)
initial (17)
innuendo (18)
insatiable (6)
insipid (2)
intercede (11)
intone (28)
inveigle (10)
inviolate (16)

iridescent (4)
itinerary (3)

JURISDICTION (17)
jurist (5)

KAYAK (19)

LACONIC (12)
lacteal (18)
laity (6)
lapidary (1)
lariat (2)
larva (10)
lattice (16)
laudatory (29)
lave (8)
layette (17)
leaven (18)
leviathan (16)
levitation (26)
lien (3)
linguist (11)
lionize (13)
listless (27)
lunar (9)
lupine (14)

MACE (1)
macerate (4)
Machiavellian (12)
madrigal (23)
maestro (2)
magniloquent (10)
malapropism (11)
malfeasance (7)
marinate (20)
marquetry (24)
marsupial (12)
masticate (10)
maudlin (11)
maxim (3)
meander (5)
melee (12)
mendacity (15)
meretricious (1)
merino (8)
mesmerize (25)

metamorphosis (30)
meteoric (2)
mien (21)
millennium (22)
milliner (26)
miscegenation (19)
misdemeanor (9)
mobilize (29)
monotheism (30)
moratorium (13)
mordant (6)
mores (4)
motif (3)

NAIAD (7)
narcotic (14)
necromancy (28)
negotiate (17)
nemesis (5)
neuter (6)
nirvana (10)
nocturne (18)
nominee (25)
nonpareil (23)
norm (4)
notary (24)
novena (15)
novitiate (5)
nugatory (11)
nullify (12)

OBITUARY (13)
objurgate (16)
oblate (24)
obliquity (29)
obsidian (30)
obtuse (20)
obviate (17)
occident (23)
octavo (10)
onomatopoeia (14)
opprobrium (6)
optimum (4)
option (18)
opulent (1)
ordinal (24)
ornithology (27)
oscillate (2)

ostensible (21)
outmoded (5)
overweening (19)

PACHYDERM (22)
palfrey (3)
panacea (16)
pandemic (23)
panegyric (8)
pantheon (11)
papal (12)
paraplegia (28)
paregoric (1)
parole (2)
parson (9)
passe' (17)
patrician (29)
patronize (30)
peroration (10)
phalanx (3)
phlegmatic (18)
physiognomy (21)
placate (24)
pleasantry (20)
plethora (11)
polemic (28)
polygamist (15)
pontificate (7)
potentate (8)
precipitate (26)
precipitous (6)
preponderate (16)
prerogative (22)
probity (4)
prognosis (21)
prognosticate (13)
proletariat (27)
promulgate (19)
propound (14)
protocol (5)
protuberant (20)
psychosis (12)
pulsate (9)
pyromaniac (7)

QUEUE (25)
quill (26)
quip (15)

quixotic (27)
quizzical (23)

RABID (29)
raconteur (13)
raffish (30)
ramifications (28)
rapport (29)
rapprochement (14)
recant (8)
reciprocate (17)
reconnaissance (18)
referendum (9)
refractory (1)
refutation (16)
regeneration (24)
reinstate (6)
repartee (22)
repine (17)
resurrect (23)
retract (30)
rheumy (2)
rift (24)
risque' (25)
roe (9)
rostrum (4)
rotund (22)
rudimentary (23)
ruminate (24)

SACHET (19)
sacrilege (10)
sapient (7)
scion (8)
sebaceous (22)
seismic (18)
sexton (20)
shroud (21)
smelt (11)
solecism (23)
sonic (26)
sophistry (28)
specious (5)
spoliation (16)
stellar (15)
sterling (12)
stoical (27)
stratagem (24)

strident (19)
subterranean (25)
suffuse (10)
sundry (22)
supposition (29)
surcease (23)
surrogate (11)
svelte (3)
sybarite (13)
symposium (9)
synopsis (12)

TACTILE (1)
talisman (14)
tariff (20)
technique (7)
temerity (8)
temperament (24)
temporize (2)
termagant (22)
tertiary (3)
threnody (26)
throes (6)

titian (17)
tocsin (1)
tonsure (18)
toreador (30)
trajectory (2)
trenchant (3)
tribulation (1)
trousseau (15)
turpitude (4)

UKASE (21)

unimpeachable (10)
unwonted (13)
upbraid (11)
utilize (12)

VACUOUS (27)
venerate (23)
venire (9)
verbose (16)
verdant (10)
vernacular (5)

vertigo (24)
vial (17)
vibrant (2)
vicissitudes (6)
viviparous (18)
vocal (11)
vortex (19)

WALLOW (20)
winsome (26)

ZENITH (12)

Introduction

This book has four main purposes: (1) to familiarize you with a large number of words (about 500) that you are likely to encounter in your reading or in various achievement tests designed to measure the extent of your vocabulary, (2) to give you a knowledge of how words are formed and how they are used, (3) to increase your ability to perform well at various kinds of vocabulary tests (entrance to college and to many occupations depends to a large extent on a person's demonstrated ability in this area), and (4) to accomplish the above in a way that you will find interesting, even enjoyable.

Each of the thirty lessons in this book has three exercises. Exercise A is designed to give you a firm grasp of the meaning or meanings of the words on the Word List. Exercise B is designed to make you familiar with how these words may and may not be used in sentences. These two exercises are the same throughout the book; Exercise C varies from lesson to lesson. Be sure to read carefully the instruction for each one.

Following each lesson is a Wordly Wise section which discusses the origin and formation of words, distinguishes between words commonly confused, provides a guide to pronunciation where needed, and generally deals with any points that may need clarification.

At the end of every third lesson there is a review of all the words in those lessons plus some review words. This is in the form of a crossword puzzle in which the clues are definitions of the words that have been studied. In order to get the most enjoyment out of these puzzles, come adequately prepared with a sure knowledge of the words covered.

Before beginning the first lesson, study the terms defined below. Refer back to this page if you encounter any of these terms and are unsure of their meanings.

Etymology is the science that studies the origins and histories of words; it is also the name given to the history of a word which shows where it came from and how it changed into its present form and meaning.

A *root* is a word or part of a word that is used as a base for making other words. The word *move* is the root of such words as re*move* and *move*ment.

A *prefix* is a syllable or group of syllables joined to the beginning of a word to change its meaning. Some common prefixes are *un-*, *non-*, *anti-*, and *in-*. In the word *remove*, *re-* is a prefix.

A *suffix* is a syllable or group of syllables added to the end of a word to change its meaning. Some common suffixes are *-able*, *-ary*, *-ful*, *-tion*. In the word *movement*, *-ment* is a suffix.

A *synonym* is a word having the same or nearly the same meaning as another word in the same language. The English *cheese* has the same meaning as the French *fromage*, but they are not synonyms. *Little* and *small* are synonyms; so are *valiant* and *brave*.

An *antonym* is a word that is opposite in meaning to another word. *Strong* and *weak* are antonyms; so are *up* and *down*.

A *homonym* is a word that is pronounced the same as another word but has a different meaning and usually a different spelling. *Hoarse* and *horse* are homonyms; so are *bow* and *bough*.

An *analogy* is a similarity in some respect between two things, it is also a comparing of something with something else. Word relationship tests make use of analogy in the following way. A pair of words is given and the relationship between them must be established. The third word must then be matched with one of a number of choices (usually four or five) to express the same kind of relationship. Here is an example:

ant is to *insect* as *robin* is to which of the following
(1) fly (2) nest (3) bird (4) sing (5) wing

The relationship between the first pair, *ant* and *insect*, is one of class; ants belong to the class of living things called insects. By selecting choice (3), we express the same kind of relationship since robins belong to the class of living things called birds. The form in which analogy questions are usually put together with the correct answer is shown here:

ant:insect :: robin:
(1) fly (2) nest (3) bird (4) sing (5) wing

Note that balance must be maintained between each pair of words. If we go from *ant* to *insect* on one side, we cannot go from *bird* to *robin* on the other as the relationship between the two pairs would not then be identical. The parts of speech of each of the two pairs must also match; *noun:verb* must be followed by *noun:verb*, *noun: adjective* by *noun:adjective* and so on.

In addition to the example given, there are many other possible relationships between words. Here are some of the more common ones:

(1) synonyms (sad:gloomy)
(2) antonyms (true:false)
(3) homonyms (rough:ruff)
(4) part:whole (page:book)
(5) worker:tool (painter:brush)
(6) worker:article produced (poet:poem)
(7) function (knife:cut)
(8) symbol (cross:Christianity)
(9) description (circle:round)
(10) size (twig:branch)
(11) lack (invalid:health)
(12) cause (germ:disease)
(13) sex (bull:cow)
(14) parent:child (mother:daughter)
(15) noun:adjective (warmth:warm)
(16) type:characteristic (cow:herbivorous)

A *metaphor* is a figure of speech in which a term or phrase is applied to something to which it is not literally applicable in order to show a likeness. The exclamation "What a pig!" would refer to a greedy person if meant metaphorically; it would refer to the animal raised for its pork and bacon if meant literally. Metaphor extends the meanings of words; *pig* has acquired its secondary meaning, "a greedy or filthy person," in this way.

To *denote* is to provide with a factual, exact definition. The word *mother* denotes a female parent. To *connote* is to suggest some feeling or idea in addition to the actual meaning. The word *mother*, to most people, connotes love, care, warmth, and tenderness.

Chapter One

Word List 1

ACETIC	EXHUME	OPULENT
CLANDESTINE	FUSILLADE	PAREGORIC
COSMIC	INFRACTION	REFRACTORY
DEVOLVE	LAPIDARY	TACTILE
EFFETE	MACE	TOCSIN
ENSEMBLE	MERETRICIOUS	TRIBULATION

Look up the words above in your dictionary. Note that many of them have more than one meaning. When you feel you know *all* the meanings of *all* the words, go on to the exercise below.

EXERCISE 1A

From the four choices following each phrase or sentence, you are to circle the letter preceding one that is closest in meaning to the italicized word. Where the same word appears more than once, you should note that it is being used in different senses.

1. *acetic* acid (a) of soil (b) of vinegar (c) of sulphur (d) of lemons

2. a *clandestine* meeting (a) open (b) private (c) secret (d) mass

3. *cosmic* theories (a) of the beginning of things (b) of time (c) of the universe (d) of the atom

4. *cosmic* distances (a) microscopic (b) varying (c) fixed (d) vast

5. to *devolve* upon (a) turn around (b) heap scorn (c) look (d) transfer

6. an *effete* nation (a) friendly (b) weak (c) ancient (d) warlike

7. to complete the *ensemble* (a) matched set of luggage (b) travel arrangements (c) obligations (d) matched outfit of clothing

8. a sense of *ensemble* (a) well-being (b) discouragement (c) failure (d) working closely together

9. a string *ensemble* (a) group of musicians (b) musical instrument (c) vibration (d) musical composition

10. to *exhume* the body (a) prepare for burial (b) bury (c) dig up (d) examine

11. to *exhume* an old play (a) revive (b) copy out (c) ridicule (d) study

12. a sudden *fusillade* (a) downpour of rain (b) fall of rock (c) firing of shots (d) mass movement of people

13. a minor *infraction* (a) form of a disease (b) breaking of a rule (c) outburst of temper (d) part in an enterprise

14. He is a *lapidary*. (a) basket weaver (b) dealer in expensive furs (c) leather worker (d) cutter of precious stones

15. a *mace*-bearer (a) chain of office (b) royal crown (c) ceremonial staff (d) train of a robe

16. to fight with a *mace* (a) spring-loaded bow (b) two-bladed ax (c) long, curved sword (d) spiked war club

17. *Mace* is a spice. (a) powdered poppy seeds (b) powdered nutmeg husks (c) dried roots of ginger (d) ground up bay leaves

18. a *meretricious* display (a) attractively designed (b) cheaply showy (c) convincing (c) poorly designed

19. *opulent* styles (a) absurd (b) unchanging (c) severe (d) luxurious

20. to take a *paregoric* (a) pain-killing drug (b) sleep-inducing drug (c) tension-reducing drug (d) appetite-reducing drug

21. a *refractory* child (a) sickly (b) bright (c) unruly (d) docile

22. a *refractory* disease (a) fatal (b) of unknown cause (c) easily cured (d) unresponsive to treatment

23. *tactile* impressions (a) from the sense of touch (b) from the sense of smell (c) from the sense of hearing (d) from the sense of taste

24. to hear the *tocsin* (a) singing bird (b) alarm bell (c) cry of fear (d) high, squeaking sound

25. a time of *tribulation* (a) uncertainty (b) prosperity (c) rejoicing (d) suffering

Check your answers against the correct ones given below. The answers are not in order; this is to prevent your eye from catching sight of the correct answers before you have had a chance to do the exercise on your own.

5d. 17b. 10c. 18b. 7d. 25d. 1b. 12c. 22d. 20a. 11a. 23a. 2c. 14d. 9a. 16d. 6b. 19d. 21c. 24b. 4d. 15c. 13b. 3c. 8d.

Look up in your dictionary all the words for which you gave incorrect answers. Only when you have done this should you go on to the next exercise.

EXERCISE 1B

Each word in Word List 1 is used several times in the following sentences to illustrate different meanings or usage. One of the sentences for each word uses the italicized word incorrectly. You are to circle the letter preceding that sentence.

1. (a) The air has turned the wine slightly *acetic.* (b) *Acetic* acid is the chief ingredient in vinegar. (c) The *acetic* life of nuns and monks is one that appeals to very few people.

2. (a) He became very *clandestine* and refused to tell us anything. (b) Police discovered a *clandestine* printing press operated by a group of revolutionaries. (c) The young lovers met *clandestinely* when their parents forbade them to see each other.

3. (a) *Cosmic* dust in minute traces is found everywhere in the universe. (b) She believes in a great *cosmic* spirit, brooding over the universe. (c) One of the major ills of the modern age is a terrible, *cosmic* boredom. (d) The mountain was so *cosmic* it took four days to reach the summit.

4. (a) On the death of the president, the position *devolves* upon the vice-president. (b) They were *devolved* of any responsibility for the accident. (c) Anarchy can result when political power *devolves* upon those not prepared for it.

5. (a) Her writing became very *effete* and lost its popular appeal. (b) The Spanish conquerers regarded the Indians of the New World as a very *effete* race. (c) We become more *effete* as we rely on gadgets to do our work for us. (d) He was able to *effete* his escape by leaving a dummy in his bed to deceive the guard.

6. (a) The actors know each other so well that a fine *ensemble* effect is created. (b) A charming, wide-brimmed hat completed his *ensemble.* (c) She played cello in a small *ensemble* for a few years before joining the symphony. (d) The actors will *ensemble* on stage in about ten minutes.

7. (a) The publisher has *exhumed* some little-known Elizabethan plays for publication soon. (b) The area around the grave was sealed off while the police *exhumed* the body. (c) We *exhumed* a few potatoes from the garden and cooked them for supper.

8. (a) They picked up their *fusillades* and fired a series of shots into the air. (b) A *fusillade* of gunfire greeted the outlaws as they rode into town. (c) She made no attempt to answer the *fusillade* of questions from the eager reporters.

9. (a) A single *infraction* of the regulations can mean dismissal from the school. (b) A large *infraction* developed in the party, but it was

not strong enough to win power. (c) To ship goods to unauthorized countries would be an *infraction* of the treaty.

10. (a) The *lapidary* cut the rough emerald into several beautifully faceted stones. (b) A course in *lapidary* is given at the evening institute for those interested in gems. (c) The *lapidary* sparkled like a diamond when held to the light.

11. (a) During the Middle Ages, the *mace*, a heavy club with spikes embedded in the end, was a fearsome weapon. (b) The lord mayor carried a *mace* as the symbol of his office. (c) The president is *maced* into office by the chief justice of the Supreme Court. (d) We added *mace* to the cake batter.

12. (a) Seaworthiness in a boat is more important than the *meretricious* attraction of newness. (b) Her *meretricious* charm was turned on and off to suit the occasion. (c) The plays he wrote were *meretricious* and are poorly regarded nowadays. (d) We boiled the water before drinking it as we were afraid it might be *meretricious*.

13. (a) A large *opulent* gleamed on the little finger of his right hand. (b) Her vast income enabled her to lead a life of *opulent* ease. (c) He was unused to such *opulence* and felt somewhat uncomfortable. (d) The magnolia puts forth *opulent* blossoms each spring.

14. (a) Tincture of opium is a *paregoric* that was once commonly used to relieve pain. (b) The doctor left a *paregoric* for the patient to take if the pain grew worse. (c) The patient became *paregoric* during the night, and a doctor was sent for.

15. (a) The horse was so *refractory* I decided not to try to ride it. (b) If the disease proves *refractory*, all the doctor can do is make the patient as comfortable as possible. (c) By

tracing the *refractory* of the bullet, the police determined from where it had been fired.

16. (a) Braille employs *tactile* symbols that can be "read" by sightless persons. (b) There was almost no *tactile* sensitivity in her calloused hands. (c) Certain forms of primitive sea life have only *tactile* contact with their environment. (d) Gold is an extremely *tactile* metal that can be drawn out into very thin wire.

17. (a) His voice rang out like a *tocsin*, calling on us to stop. (b) The *tocsin* was sounded at the first sight of the raiders. (c) A sharp rise in prices is a *tocsin* that we ignore at our peril. (d) Carbon monoxide is extremely *tocsin* and has been the cause of many deaths.

18. (a) After many *tribulations* Columbus returned to Spain with news of his great discovery. (b) The captive nations were forced to pay *tribulation* to their conquerer. (c) The book recaptures all the *tribulations* faced by the factory workers.

EXERCISE 1C

Each of the italicized words in the sentences below is used either literally or metaphorically (explanations of these terms are given in the Introduction). In the appropriate space, write *L* if the word is used literally, write *M* if it is used metaphorically.

1. The motor *died* (   ) as soon as I took my foot off the gas pedal.

2. The roads are *icy* (   ), so please drive carefully.

3. My grandfather *died* (   ) at the age of ninety-two.

4. She is a very *shallow* (   ) person.

5. The sailboat came to a stop as soon as the wind *died* (   ).

6. A *volley* (   ) of oaths greeted us when we returned.

7. Her *icy* (   ) stare made me feel very uncomfortable.

8. The body was laid to rest in a *shallow* (   ) grave.

9. Who *broke* (   ) the vase?

10. The reporters fired a *volley* (   ) of questions at him.

11. You *broke* (   ) your promise not to reveal my whereabouts.

12. The soldiers fired a *volley* (   ) of shots at the retreating figures of the enemy.

13. Codfish are abundant in the *icy* (   ) waters off the coast of Greenland.

14. The water is quite *shallow* (   ) around the edges of the lake.

15. He *broke* (   ) his back in a fall from the roof.

16. He *broke* (   ) his fall when he landed in the pile of hay.

WORDLY WISE 1

ACETIC (pronounced ∂-SEET-ik) refers to the sharp, sour liquid (acetic acid) found in vinegar. Don't confuse this word with *ascetic* (pronounced ∂-SET-ik), which means "rigorously self-denying" (the ascetic life of a saint). The symbol ∂ indicates pronunciation of the letter *a* in *about* and *ago*.

DEVOLVE is invariably followed by *on* or *upon* (the responsibility devolved *upon* me).

Note that LAPIDARY refers both to the art of gem cutting and to the gem cutter (a lapidary is an expert in lapidary).

Etymology (See the Introduction for an explanation of this term, together with the notes on roots, prefixes, and suffixes.)

Study the roots and prefixes given above together with the English words derived from them. Capitalized words are those given in the Word List. You should look up in a dictionary any words that are unfamiliar to you.

Prefixes: *ex-* (out) Latin — Examples: *EX*HUME, *ex*cavate, *ex*ile

de- (down) Latin — Examples: *DE*VOLVE, *de*cline, *de*press

Roots: *fract* (break) Latin — Examples: RE*FRACT*ORY, *fract*ure, re*fract*

lapis (stone) Latin — Examples: *LAPI*DARY, di*lapid*ated, *lapis* lazuli

---

Word List 2

ANIMALCULE	FOMENT	OSCILLATE
COLLATERAL	IMPEACH	PAROLE
DEFRAY	INSIPID	RHEUMY
DISCONSOLATE	LARIAT	TEMPORIZE
EMERITUS	MAESTRO	TRAJECTORY
EQUABLE	METEORIC	VIBRANT

Look up the words above in your dictionary. Note that many of them have more than one meaning. When you feel you know *all* the meanings of *all* the words, go on to the exercise below.

EXERCISE 2A

From the four choices following each phrase or sentence, you are to circle the letter preceding the one that is closest in meaning to the italicized word. Where the same word appears more than once, you should note that it is being used in different senses.

1. to study the *animalcule* (a) ancient animal remains (b) microscopic life form (c) track left by an animal (d) animal disease

2. to provide *collateral* (a) security for a loan (b) evidence in a trial (c) protection against attack (d) proof of one's good intentions

3. *collateral* evidence (a) faked (b) irrelevant (c) irrefutable (d) supporting

4. *collateral* relatives (a) in direct line of descent

(b) joined together by marriage (c) quarrelsome (d) of a separate line of descent

5. to *defray* the cost (a) pay (b) reduce (c) question (d) fail to pay

6. to be *disconsolate* (a) terribly angry (b) extremely happy (c) very sad (d) unsteady on one's feet

7. a professor *emeritus* (a) who is newly appointed to that position (b) who has retired but keeps his or her rank (c) who is the head of a department (d) who holds a doctor's degree in a particular subject

8. an *equable* climate (a) near the equator (b) unchanging (c) uncertain (d) cold

9. to *foment* a riot (a) break up (b) stir up (c) take part in (d) lead

10. to *impeach* an official (a) offer bribes to (b) charge with a crime (c) help to elect (d) win the support of

11. to *impeach* her honor (a) free from doubt concerning (b) praise (c) appeal to (d) raise doubts concerning

12. an *insipid* brew (a) vile tasting (b) mysterious (c) thick (d) tasteless

13. an *insipid* speech (a) uninspiring (b) in bad taste (c) angry (d) unrehearsed

14. a cowboy's *lariat* (a) tall, broad-brimmed hat (b) rope used to catch cattle and horses (c) leather covering to protect the legs (d) iron used to brand cattle

15. to greet the *maestro* (a) military leader (b) head of state (c) master musician (d) bearer of good news

16. a *meteoric* rise (a) slow (b) delayed (c) swift (d) uninterrupted

17. a *meteoric* shower (a) of tropical rain (b) of white-hot sparks (c) of shooting stars (d) of icy water

18. to cause something to *oscillate* (a) gradually increase in size (b) gradually decrease in size (c) continually revolve (d) swing back and forth

19. to ask for *parole* (a) pardon for one's crimes (b) early release from prison (c) the dropping of criminal charges (d) review of a case by a higher court

20. *rheumy* eyes (a) sightless (b) large (c) sparkling (d) watering

21. forced to *temporize* (a) stall for time (b) yield to another's demands (c) take strong measures (d) go too fast

22. Don't *temporize*! (a) judge before all the facts are known (b) act merely to suit the immediate moment (c) give way to sudden fits of temper (d) be excessively harsh and unyielding

23. the *trajectory* of the bullet (a) speed (b) killing power (c) curved path (d) diameter

24. a *vibrant* person (a) energetic (b) nervous (c) excited (d) dull

25. *vibrant* tones (a) quavering (b) piping (c) rich (d) warbling

26. a *vibrant* wire (a) quivering (b) taut (c) slack (d) looped

Check your answers against the correct ones given on the next page. The answers are not in order; this is to prevent your eye from catching

5

sight of the correct answers before you have had a chance to do the exercise on your own.

5a. 17c. 10b. 18d. 7b. 25c. 1b. 12d. 22b. 20d. 11d. 23c. 2a. 14b. 9b. 26a. 16c. 6c. 19b. 21a. 24a. 4d. 15c. 13a. 3d. 8b.

Look up in your dictionary all the words for which you gave incorrect answers. Only when you have done this should you go on to the next exercise.

EXERCISE 2B

Each word in Word List 2 is used several times in the sentences below to illustrate different meanings or usage. One of the sentences for each word uses the italicized word incorrectly. You are to circle the letter preceding that sentence.

1. (a) The microscope reveals countless *animalcules* in a single drop of ditchwater. (b) The amoeba is an extremely *animalcule* creature.

2. (a) They offered some government bonds as *collateral* for the loan. (b) The statements made by the accused after the arrest are *collateral* evidence and probably will not be used in the trial. (c) Where there is no lineal descendent, a nobleman's title may go to a *collateral* relative. (d) The design on the medal was in the shape of a *collateral*.

3. (a) She offered to *defray* our expenses. (b) The hikers looked terribly *defrayed* as though they hadn't slept for a week.

4. (a) She looked so *disconsolate* when I refused that I was forced to change my mind. (b) Unable to get him to change his mind, we returned *disconsolately* to our homes. (c) He plugged in the small *disconsolate* he had brought with him.

5. (a) For many years until her retirement she was an *emeritus* in the physics department. (b) Doctor Stein is professor *emeritus* of history at the state university. (c) Upon her retirement the president of the college was granted the title of president *emeritus*.

6. (a) We preferred a more *equable* climate to the hot summers and cold winters of Maine. (b) Our dog has an *equable* temperament and never gets excited. (c) They complained that the money had not been shared on an *equable* basis.

7. (a) His speech was bound to *foment* discussion in the club. (b) The entire state was in a *foment* on election day. (c) They have been traveling around the country *fomenting* riots in the cities.

8. (a) The senator was so angry he threatened to have the chief justice *impeached*. (b) The *impeachment* of President Andrew Johnson resulted in his being cleared of the charges brought against him. (c) The defense lawyer tried to *impeach* the honesty of the witness for the prosecution. (d) The wool is *impeached* in a chemical solution before it is sent for spinning.

9. (a) The water must be *insipid*, neither too hot nor too cold. (b) I thought the vegetables, overcooked and watery, particularly *insipid*. (c) Gambling, which had once been the most exciting of pastimes, now seemed *insipid* to him. (d) Her *insipid* manner is not one to arouse great enthusiasm among her followers.

10. (a) The cowboy twirled his *lariat* in a skillful display of roping steers. (b) The cowgirl dropped the *lariat* skillfully over the head of the steer. (c) The rope the farmer used to tie the steer was made of strong *lariat*.

11. (a) The orchestra was conducted with great *maestro* by the young conductor. (b) She wrote a book on the great conductor Arturo Toscanini that deals with the *maestro's* later years. (c) The members of the orchestra rose to their feet as the *maestro* entered.

12. (a) Her rise in the tennis world was *meteoric*—winner at Wimbledon at sixteen, winner at Forest Hills at eighteen. (b) The craters on the moon are believed to be *meteoric* in origin. (c) A *meteoric* entering the earth's

atmosphere is rapidly burned up. (d) *Meteoric* showers are seen when swarms of meteors enter the earth's atmosphere as shooting stars.

13. (a) The pendulum of the clock *oscillates* through a fifteen-degree arc. (b) Public opinion *oscillates* between the extremes of high optimism and despair. (c) The *oscillate* made a clicking sound as it swung from side to side. (d) Charts record the *oscillations* of climate as it changes from drought to heavy rainfall and back again.

14. (a) After serving one third of their sentences, prisoners are eligible for *parole*. (b) A condition of her release from prison was that she visit her *parole* officer weekly. (c) The two young *paroles* were warned to stay out of trouble to avoid returning to prison. (d) People on *parole* can be returned to prison if they break the conditions of their release.

15. (a) The sniffles and *rheumy* eyes of the children showed that they all had colds. (b) The best treatment for *rheumy* is a couple of aspirins and lots of fluids.

16. (a) He tried to *temporize*, hoping that by the next day the situation would be clearer. (b) She tried to *temporize* the people by saying that she would help them. (c) They should stop *temporizing* and do what is right rather than what is to their immediate advantage.

17. (a) Computers plot the *trajectory* of the rocket from firing to the moment of impact. (b) By tracing the *trajectory* of the bullet, police discovered the window from which it had been fired. (c) The *trajectory* struck the target slightly high and to the left.

18. (a) Her *vibrant* voice has thrilled audiences all over the world. (b) The message was flashed along the *vibrant* wires of the telegraph. (c) He was a noted *vibrant*, a lover of good food and fine wines. (d) The Elizabethan age was *vibrant* with the excitement of discovery.

EXERCISE 2C

In each of the sentences below a word is omitted. From the four words provided, select and fill in the one that best completes the sentence. Allow five minutes for this test. If you cannot answer a question, go on to the next one without delay. If you have time left over at the end, go back and try to fill in unanswered questions.

9 or over correct:	excellent
7 to 8 correct:	good
6 or under correct:	thorough review of A exercises indicated

1. The wine had turned somewhat . . . . and was unfit for drinking.
effete rheumy acetic tactile

2. I offered to help . . . . their expenses.
devolve defray parole impeach

3. The . . . . was rung to warn the village of the raid.
animalcule trajectory parole tocsin

4. A large diamond pin lent the finishing touch to her . . . .
effete paregoric ensemble emeritus

5. A . . . . of shots greeted the riders as they approached the town.
collateral trajectory fusillade tribulation

6. If the president dies in office, the position . . . . upon the vice-president.
defrays devolves impeaches exhumes

7. The police will . . . . the body for they suspect the person was murdered.
exhume clandestine ensemble defray

8. The police were able to trace the . . . . of the bullet.
oscillate collateral fusillade trajectory

9. On his retirement from full-time teaching, he was made professor . . . .
maestro emeritus lapidary collateral

10. The . . . . promised to have the emerald cut and set into the brooch.

lapidary mace paregoric maestro

WORDLY WISE 2

EQUABLE means "unchanging; steady; even" (an equable climate). *Equitable* means "fair; just" (an equitable price). Both words derive from the Latin *aequus* (even).

MAESTRO (pronounced *MYS-tro*) is an Italian word, as are most of our musical terms, and means "master." It is a title of honor used to describe only a few who have achieved great eminence in the world of music; when used in other contexts, it gives a somewhat humorous coloration to the word.

Etymology

Study the roots and prefix given below, together with the English words derived from them. Capitalized words are those given in the Word List. You should look up in a dictionary any words that are unfamiliar to you.

Prefix: *trans-* (across) Latin — Examples: TRA-JECTORY, *trans*port, *trans*it

Roots: *tempus* (time) Latin — Examples: TEM-PORIZE, *tempo*rary, *tempo*

jacere (throw) Latin — Examples: TRA-JECTORY, e*ject*, pro*ject*

Word List 3

ASPHYXIATE	FRIEZE	PALFREY
CORNUCOPIA	INDITE	PHALANX
DESIST	ITINERARY	SVELTE
EFFEMINATE	LIEN	TERTIARY
EMPATHY	MAXIM	TRENCHANT
EVANESCENT	MOTIF	

Look up the words above in your dictionary. Note that many of them have more than one meaning. When you feel you know *all* the meanings of *all* the words, go on to the following exercise.

EXERCISE 3A

From the four choices following each phrase or sentence, you are to circle the letter preceding the one that is closest in meaning to the italicized word. Where the same word appears more than once, you should note that it is being used in different senses.

1. to *asphyxiate* someone (a) make unconscious through loss of blood (b) make partially or totally paralyzed (c) make unconscious by cutting off the supply of oxygen (d) lower the bodily temperature of

2. a decorative *cornucopia* (a) float in a parade (b) triumphal arch (c) Greek column (d) horn of plenty

3. a *cornucopia* of good things (a) deeply-felt need (b) surprise package (c) limited supply (d) inexhaustible supply

4. told to *desist* (a) stop (b) start (c) slow down (d) keep trying

5. an *effeminate* manner (a) graceful (b) woman-like (c) hesitant (d) firm

6. to achieve *empathy* (a) a victory over a personal handicap (b) an ambition of long standing (c) a feeling of sharing another's emotions or experiences (d) an understanding of oneself

7. *evanescent* pleasures (a) stolen (b) sinful (c) secret (d) fleeting

8. *evanescent* brushwork (a) impermanent (b) heavy (c) colorful (d) delicate

9. a long *frieze* (a) embroidered Indian robe (b) ornamental band on a wall (c) line of ornamental trees or shrubs (d) fortified embankment

10. to *indite* a message (a) read (b) remember (c) write (d) forget

11. to *indite* a poem (a) learn by heart (b) set to music (c) recite (d) compose

12. the president's *itinerary* (a) list of appointments (b) group of advisers (c) planned route (d) term of office

13. to have a *lien* (a) right to buy property at a fixed price (b) period of grace in which to make a payment (c) legal claim to a debtor's property (d) loan for which property is offered as security

14. to remember the *maxim* (a) solution to a riddle or puzzle (b) concisely-stated rule of conduct (c) meaning of a poem (d) method of solving a mathematical problem

15. the main *motif* (a) speech (b) theme (c) character (d) plot

16. a black *palfrey* (a) riding horse (b) hunting dog (c) prison cell (d) leather jacket

17. a *phalanx* of soldiers (a) vast army (b) single file (c) thin line (d) massed group

18. a *svelte* figure (a) heavily overweight (b) gracefully slender (c) shapeless (d) gaunt and thin

19. a *svelte* manner (a) cold (b) hearty (c) secretive (d) sophisticated

20. a *tertiary* characteristic (a) first in importance (b) second in importance (c) third in importance (d) fourth in importance

21. a *trenchant* writer (a) sloppily sentimental (b) deceptively simple (c) deliberately obscure (d) vigorously expressive

Check your answers against the correct ones given below. The answers are not in order; this is to prevent your eye from catching sight of the correct answers before you have had a chance to do the exercise on your own.

12c. 3d. 15b. 8d. 17d. 16a. 18b. 2d. 11d. 21d. 4a. 10c. 14b. 13c. 5b. 20c. 7d. 1c. 6c. 19d. 9b.

Look up in your dictionary all the words for which you gave incorrect answers. Only when you have done this should you go on to the next exercise.

EXERCISE 3B

Each word in Word List 3 is used several times in the sentences below to illustrate different meanings or usage. One of the sentences for each word uses the italicized word incorrectly. You are to circle the letter preceding that sentence.

1. (a) The woman in the garage was *asphyxiated* by the carbon monoxide fumes from the car. (b) A baby putting its head into a plastic bag can easily *asphyxiate* itself. (c) The navigator could *asphyxiate* the ship's position by checking the stars.

2. (a) A *cornucopia*, or ram's horn filled to overflowing with things to eat, makes a fine decorative piece. (b) The settlers planted *cornucopia* in the land they cleared. (c) Car lovers regard Detroit as a veritable *cornucopia* of glittering automobiles.

3. (a) She promised to *desist* from meddling in the affairs of others. (b) His hand shook so much as he tried to shave that he was forced to *desist*. (c) The brakes are worn out and can barely *desist* the carriage even when they are completely engaged.

4. (a) Criticizing him for having an *effeminate* manner is quite narrowminded of you. (b) A French noun can be masculine, *effeminate*, or neuter. (c) His *effeminate* manner seemed to antagonize some people.

5. (a) Most parents feel a deep *empathy* with their babies. (b) The printed page creates an *empathy* between the author and the reader. (c) This novelist, by her skillful portrayal of character, helps us feel *empathy* with people we ordinarily might dislike. (d) They received many expressions of *empathy* when their father died.

6. (a) The sun's warmth soon scattered the *evanescent* wisps of mist on the mountain. (b) Her moods of depression are *evanescent*, and she is soon laughing again. (c) In the *evanescent* landscapes of Turner, English painting reached its peak. (d) They grew more and more

evanescent as they got older, preferring to be completely alone.

7. (a) A *frieze* decorated the walls of the villa. (b) The *frieze,* carved with great delicacy, shows various hunting and woodland scenes. (c) The artist has tried to *frieze* the figures in the design into everyday attitudes.

8. (a) Challenged to compose a poem on the spur of the moment, Keats *indited* the lovely sonnet beginning "The poetry of earth is never dead." (b) Picking up a pen, she commenced to *indite* a letter to her friend. (c) After being *indited* for murder, the prisoner was led back to the cell.

9. (a) We made a careful *itinerary* of everything we might need. (b) The queen's *itinerary* for her round-the-world trip was released today. (c) Our *itinerary* takes us through the Canadian Rockies and into Idaho and Oregon.

10. (a) The bank has a *lien* on the property because of the money owed it by the owner. (b) She took out a *lien* on her house for five thousand dollars. (c) You cannot sell your car if your creditor has a *lien* on it.

11. (a) "Better late than never" is a *maxim* that should be applied with caution. (b) Each of the fables of Aesop illustrates a *maxim* for our guidance. (c) They hope to *maxim* their profits by cutting costs and raising prices.

12. (a) Throughout the novel runs the *motif* of the son seeking his father. (b) This simple four-note *motif* runs through the entire symphony. (c) The material was decorated with a tasteful leaf *motif*. (d) No *motif* for the crime has been discovered by the police.

13. (a) The young girl, mounted on a gray *palfrey*, made her way through the forest. (b) The horses were taught to *palfrey* proudly through the forest. (c) The queen rode a spirited charger while the king was mounted on a docile *palfrey*.

14. (a) The emperor wore a *phalanx* of solid gold across his breast. (b) The soldiers of Philip of Macedon were organized into *phalanxes* eight rows deep. (c) The police officers formed a solid *phalanx* and charged in through the door.

15. (a) After losing twenty-five extra pounds, he looked very *svelte* in his new clothes. (b) Her *svelte* manner impressed many people at the meeting. (c) It grew so *svelte* in the room that we opened all the windows.

16. (a) Her first two attempts failed, but her *tertiary* attempt succeeded. (b) Two primary colors make a secondary color; two secondary colors make a *tertiary* color. (c) A *tertiary* layer is sometimes put on over the primary and secondary layers.

17. (a) Her *trenchant* criticism of the government aroused the wrath of those in office. (b) He has an overpowering *trenchant* for fruit and eats some with every meal. (c) She has a *trenchant* wit that penetrates like a sharp blade.

EXERCISE 3C

This exercise is designed to enable you to find out how quickly and accurately you can handle questions using synonyms (an explanation of synonyms is given in the Introduction). It also tests how well you have learned the vocabulary words covered so far.

Underline the word which is most similar in meaning to the capitalized word. Allow ten minutes only for this test. If you cannot answer a question, go on to the next one without delay. If you have time left over at the end, go back and try to fill in unanswered questions.

22 or over correct:	excellent
17 – 21 correct:	good
16 or under correct:	thorough review of A exercises indicated

1. SAYING
   motif parole maxim cornucopia lien

2. ENERGETIC
   refractory vibrant clandestine opulent paregoric

3. FLEETING
   clandestine disconsolate evanescent meretricious refractory

4. WRITE
   desist parole defray impeach indite

5. UNRULY
   clandestine equable rheumy refractory acetic

6. SUFFOCATE
   oscillate exhume asphyxiate foment devolve

7. OUTFIT
   palfrey ensemble tocsin motif collateral

8. SECURITY
   collateral paregoric lapidary emeritus tertiary

9. STOP
   devolve defray parole palfrey desist

10. SECRET
    refractory trenchant clandestine itinerary evanescent

11. THEME
    frieze phalanx tocsin motif maxim

12. WEAK
    paregoric acetic effete tactile emeritus

13. UNCHANGING
    equable effete insipid opulent vibrant

14. PAY
    foment oscillate desist temporize defray

15. RICH
    equable collateral meretricious lapidary opulent

16. SAD
    lapidary cosmic clandestine disconsolate svelte

17. SWING
    trajectory phalanx empathy defray oscillate

18. ROUTE
    itinerary infraction ensemble clandestine trajectory

19. SLENDER
    svelte collateral emeritus evanescent trenchant

20. SHOWY
    vibrant meretricious tertiary refractory effete

21. INCITE
    ensemble disconsolate frieze foment indite

22. WOMANLIKE
    emeritus effeminate lapidary insipid refractory

23. DELAY
    devolve desist temporize tactile foment

24. SUFFERING
    tribulation cornucopia maxim tocsin phalanx

25. TASTELESS
    tactile acetic insipid cosmic lapidary

WORDLY WISE 3

EFFEMINATE has been used to describe actions or qualities in a man which used to be attributed to and expected only in a woman. (His hands had an almost effeminate softness.) *Feminine* means "pertaining to a woman." (Some people think feminine fashions are changed so often in order to make more money for the clothing industry.) These two words have quite different applications and should not be confused.

Sympathy is a general term, ranging in meaning from friendly interest or agreement (I am in sympathy with your aims) to strong emotional attachment or deep tenderness (they showed great sympathy when my mother died). EMPATHY is a narrower term and means the ability to project oneself into the emotional or intellectual processes of another (the empathy between the child learning to swim and the woman teaching him).

INDITE means "to set down on paper" (to indite a message). *Indict* means "to charge with a crime" (indicted for armed robbery). These two words are pronounced in the same way (*in-DYT*).

Etymology

Study the roots given below together with the English words derived from them. Capitalized words are those given in the Word List. You should look up in a dictionary any words that are unfamiliar to you.

Roots: *pathos* (feeling) Greek — Examples: EM*PATHY*, sym*pathy*, *path*etic
cornu (horn) Latin — Examples: *CORNU*-COPIA, uni*corn*, *corn*et
copia (plenty) Latin — Examples: *copi*ous, CORNU*COPIA*

The crossword puzzle for this first chapter has fifty-three clues. Each clue is a definition of a word from Word List 1, 2, or 3. Unless otherwise stated, a word is always used in the form in which it appears on the Word List; each word is used only once.

For every crossword puzzle after the first, review words are included. These are indicated by the number of the Word List from which they are taken appearing after the clue.

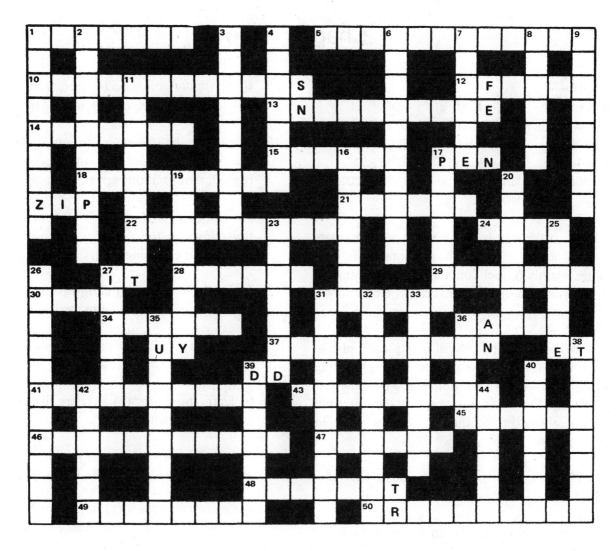

ACROSS

1. having to do with the sense of touch
5. extremely unhappy
10. cheaply gaudy; flashy
12. weak; lacking vitality
13. a microscopic life form
14. wealthy; well-endowed
15. a looped rope used for catching horses, etc.
18. to swing back and forth
21. the early release of a prisoner on condition of good behavior
22. to make or become unconscious through lack of oxygen
24. a staff used as a symbol of office
28. to cease; to stop
29. a feeling of shared emotion
30. a legal claim on the property of a debtor
31. watery (eyes or nose) because of a cold
34. to pay costs or expenses
36. a concisely stated rule of conduct
37. a breaking of a rule or law
41. womanlike; acting like a woman
43. a medicine that relieves pain
45. to excite or stir up
46. great misery or distress
47. an alarm bell; a warning
48. full of energy
49. a sense of working together harmoniously
50. the curved path of something propelled through space

DOWN

1. to be evasive in order to gain time
2. an inexhaustible supply
3. a route one travels or plans to travel
4. changing little; even
6. security for a loan
7. slender and graceful
8. of or relating to the acid in vinegar
9. retired but keeping one's rank
11. vigorously expressive; sharply worded
16. to charge with crime in office
17. a docile riding horse
19. a cutter and polisher of precious stones
20. a closely-massed group
23. lacking flavor; tasteless
25. to remove (a dead body) from a grave
26. marked by or conducted in secrecy
27. to set down in writing
31. hard to handle; unruly
32. of short duration; fleeting
33. brilliant and rapid in ascending
35. a simultaneous firing of many guns
36. a recurring feature; a theme
38. third in order
39. to pass to another; to transfer
40. a great artist, especially a master musician
42. an ornamental band around a wall
44. pertaining to the universe; vast

Chapter Two

Word List 4

ABORTIVE	EMPIRICAL	NORM
ANOMALOUS	EXCULPATE	OPTIMUM
CAPTIOUS	FIRMAMENT	PROBITY
COADJUTOR	IRIDESCENT	ROSTRUM
DISJOINTED	MACERATE	TURPITUDE
EDUCE	MORES	

Look up the words above in your dictionary. Note that many of them have more than one meaning. When you feel you know *all* the meanings of *all* the words go on to the exercise below.

EXERCISE 4A

From the four choices following each phrase or sentence, you are to circle the letter preceding the one that is closest in meaning to the italicized word. Where the same word appears more than once, you should note that it is being used in different senses.

1. an *abortive* attempt (a) successful (b) half-hearted (c) unsuccessful (d) determined

2. an *anomalous* position (a) irregular (b) exposed (c) secure (d) comfortable

3. *captious* comments (a) helpful (b) confidential (c) written (d) unduly critical

4. *captious* objections (a) deeply felt (b) legal (c) argumentative (d) serious

5. one's *coadjutor* (a) assistant (b) judge (c) superior (d) accuser

6. *disjointed* remarks (a) disparaging (b) disconnected (c) disagreeable (d) disheartening

7. to *educe* a conclusion (a) question (b) disprove (c) propose (d) arrive at

8. *empirical* proof (a) based on theory (b) based on observation (c) not verifiable (d) logically reasoned

9. to *exculpate* someone (a) free from blame (b) put to death (c) reject (d) heap scorn upon

10. to gaze at the *firmament* (a) monument to the war dead (b) dome of the sky (c) sea (d) rugged, mountainous terrain

11. an *iridescent* surface (a) of deepest black (b) that glows in the dark (c) that reflects light back (d) of changing colors

12. to *macerate* foods (a) chop up (b) soften in a liquid (c) preserve (d) whip until stiff

13. a *macerated* body (a) bruised (b) wasted away (c) sunburned (d) muscular

14. to learn the *mores* (a) answers (b) reasons (c) methods (d) customs

15. What is the *norm*? (a) chief purpose (b) reason given (c) end result (d) standard applied

16. *optimum* conditions (a) hoped for (b) average (c) most favorable (d) unchanged

17. a person of great *probity* (a) honesty (b) wisdom (c) ability (d) generosity

18. to ascend the *rostrum* (a) platform used in a hanging (b) platform used for speechmaking (c) ship's rope ladder (d) throne that is borne aloft

19. They admitted their *turpitude.* (a) terrible mistake (b) vileness of conduct (c) criminal record (d) inability to pay

Check your answers against the correct ones given below. The answers are not in order; this is to prevent your eye from catching sight of the correct answers before you have had a chance to do the exercise on your own.

12b. 3d. 15d. 8b. 17a. 16c. 18b. 2a. 11d. 4c. 10b. 14d. 13b. 5a. 7d. 1c. 6b. 19b. 9a.

Look up in your dictionary all the words for which you gave incorrect answers. Only when you have done this should you go on to the next exercise.

EXERCISE 4B

Each word in Word List 4 is used several times in the sentences below to illustrate different meanings or usage. One of the sentences for each word uses the italicized word incorrectly. You are to circle the letter preceding that sentence.

1. (a) After several *abortive* attempts to get the kite aloft, they gave up. (b) The engineer was prepared to *abortive* the rocket launch if anything went wrong.

2. (a) The team is in the *anomalous* position of being ranked first in the world and only second in its own country. (b) The penguin is an *anomaly* among birds in that it is unable to fly. (c) The author preferred to remain *anomalous* and used the name "John Doe." (d) She discussed the *anomalous* position of the free Negro in a slave state.

3. (a) Try to be less *captious* and more helpful in your criticism. (b) The land was rocky and *captious* with hardly anything growing on it. (c) Most of her questions were *captious*, designed to confuse the witness rather than to obtain information.

4. (a) He was invited to *coadjutor* the talent contest being held that afternoon. (b) The Nobel prize winner in physics said that her *coadjutors* should share the prize with her. (c) The bishop and his *coadjutor* finished their duties before the service began.

5. (a) She writes such short, *disjointed* sentences that it is hard to follow her thoughts. (b) I tried to listen to their conversation but caught just a few *disjointed* remarks. (c) The members felt *disjointed* at not being asked for their views on the new plan.

6. (a) They were *educed* into parting with all their money by two smooth-talking swindlers.

(b) What can the politican *educe* from the latest public opinion polls? (c) No firm conclusions are *educible* from the information available. (d) From the mass of data she was able to *educe* several important principles for her book.

7. (a) She is an *empiricist* and has no patience with vague theories. (b) The theory has been supported by a number of *empirical* observations. (c) *Empiricism* is a branch of philosophy that bases its conclusions on observation and experiment. (d) Caesar returned in triumph to the *empirical* city of Rome.

8. (a) The woman was accused of being an *exculpate* from justice. (b) The court *exculpated* him and dropped all charges against him. (c) Although they were not convicted, they cannot wholly be *exculpated* from involvement in the crime.

9. (a) Contact with spaceships can be lost when they go through clouds of *firmament*. (b) Her telescope scanned the starry *firmament* every night. (c) The Bible tells how God made the *firmament* and sprinkled it with stars. (d) As the sun dropped below the horizon, the *firmament* changed from blue to purple.

10. (a) The article speaks of the *iridescent* quality of oil slicks on water. (b) They had the *iridescent* set into a brooch which they gave to their eldest daughter. (c) The material was *iridescent*, now blue-green, now gray, now blue-green again. (d) the *iridescence* of the water beetle, with the shimmering, constantly-changing color is one of Nature's marvels.

11. (a) Cancer can cause severe *maceration* of the body. (b) The opposing team was *macerated* by us, the score being 36 to 0. (c) The flax is too stiff to be used in its natural state, so it is *macerated* in water. (d) His *macerated* body was evidence that he had gone without food for many days.

12. (a) Anthropologists often study the *mores* of societies different from their own. (b) Decorating a fir tree for Christmas is a *more* that

originated in Germany. (c) Visitors to unfamiliar countries must be careful not to offend against the *mores* of the local inhabitants.

13. (a) Some children have I.Q.s of over 130, but 110 is the *norm* in this group. (b) If you want to get into a good college, you will have to score well above the national *norm*. (c) Her temperature returned to *norm* after a few hours. (d) In setting up the experiment, we first had to establish what were the *norms*.

14. (a) The conditions that will produce the *optimum* amount of profit are not easy to calculate. (b) Under *optimum* conditions, the plants are ready for harvesting in forty days. (c) The *optimum* forecast was that we would be trapped in the cave for at least two days.

15. (a) A government *probity* into the sale of mining stocks is being launched immediately. (b) His *probity* is unquestioned, and no one seriously believes he was involved in the theft. (c) They say that persons of the highest *probity* are accepted into the ranks of the F. B. I.

16. (a) The speaker pounded the *rostrum* in an attempt to silence the shouts of the crowd. (b) Each speaker was allowed ten minutes at the *rostrum* to explain his position. (c) A wild *rostrum*, in which several people were injured, broke out during the meeting.

17. (a) Her admitted *turpitude* makes her an unfit person for this position. (b) Persons guilty of moral *turpitude* may not be admitted to this country. (c) He cleaned the parts with *turpitude* before putting them back together.

EXERCISE 4C

Two common Latin roots are *fra(n)g* (occurring in some words as *fract*), which means "break," and *fac(t)*, which mean "make." Add appropriate suffixes to these roots to construct words matching the following definitions.

1. _____ a building or buildings where goods are manufactured

2. _____ a break, especially of a bone

3. _____ one who transacts business for others

4. _____ easily broken

5. _____ a quantity less than a whole number

6. _____ one hired to do various kinds of work

7. _____ a part broken away

8. _____ an exact copy or reproduction

9. _____ to make easier

10. _____ produced artificially

WORDLY WISE 4

Note that MORES (pronounced *MOR-aze*), meaning "customs," occurs only in plural form. We can speak of a strange custom but not of a strange more.

Be clear as to the distinction between OPTIMUM and *maximum*. An optimum speed would be the best one under any given set of conditions; for greatest fuel economy, a car's optimum might be 35 m.p.h. A maximum speed is the greatest possible; the same car might have a maximum speed of over 100 m.p.h.

Word List 5

ACCOLADE	ERUPT	NOVITIATE
ANTIPATHY	FELICITOUS	OUTMODED
CARMINE	INFLECT	PROTOCOL
COALESCE	JURIST	SPECIOUS
DISSIMULATE	MEANDER	VERNACULAR
EGOTISM	NEMESIS	

Look up the words above in your dictionary. Note that many of them have more than one meaning. When you feel that you know *all* the meanings of *all* the words, go on to the following exercises.

From the four choices following each phrase or sentence, you are to circle the letter preceding the one that is closest in meaning to the italicized word. Where the same word appears more than once, you should note that it is being used in different senses.

1. to receive an *accolade* (a) severe scolding (b) award of merit (c) sum of money on retiring (d) ambassador from a foreign state

2. a look of *antipathy* (a) dislike (b) indifference (c) anticipation (d) warmth

3. *carmine* lips (a) thin (b) red (c) cruel (d) thick

4. to *coalesce* slowly (a) separate (b) come together (c) burn up (d) harden

5. to *dissimulate* (a) disagree violently (b) pretend to be dead (c) become impatient (d) hide one's true feelings

6. accused of *egotism* (a) holding views contrary to those officially taught (b) fomenting rebellion (c) unnecessarily risking the safety of others (d) having too high an opinion of oneself

7. to *erupt* suddenly (a) burst forth (b) collapse (c) change direction (d) stop

8. to treat the *eruption* (a) skin rash (b) broken bone (c) burst blood vessel (d) open cut

9. *felicitous* remarks (a) jealous (b) deliberately provocative (c) angry (d) pleasingly appropriate

10. a *felicitous* climate (a) hot (b) cold (c) severe (d) delightful

11. to *inflect* the voice (a) change the pitch of (b) throw forward (c) train (d) throw to another part of the room

12. to *inflect* a word (a) break down (b) say distinctly (c) spell out (d) change the form of

13. a famous *jurist* (a) expert on music (b) expert on law (c) expert on war (d) expert on painting

14. The river *meanders*. (a) winds back and forth (b) drops rapidly (c) narrows (d) flows quickly

15. to *meander* across (a) saunter (b) hurry (c) creep (d) march

16. This was his *nemesis*. (a) masterpiece (b) devilish plan (c) sole responsibility (d) revenging agent

17. to escape *nemesis* (a) unscathed (b) by the skin of one's teeth (c) just punishment (d) one to whom money is owed

18. a young *novitiate* (a) warrior (b) beginner (c) athlete (d) leader

19. to complete one's *novitiate* (a) series of assigned tasks (b) life's work (c) work of art acknowledged as one's greatest (d) probationary period in a religious order

20. *outmoded* ideas (a) outlandish (b) outdated (c) outrageous (d) outlawed

21. to learn the *protocol* (a) secret plan (b) mathematical proof (c) diplomatic etiquette (d) secret code

22. to read the *protocol* (a) book of etiquette (b) invitation to an official reception (c) list of official guests (d) original draft of a document

23. *specious* reasoning (a) seemingly true but actually false (b) building on what has been already established (c) seemingly incorrect but actually correct (d) based on observation rather than theory

24. in the *vernacular* (a) unusual circumstances (b) everyday speech (c) uncharted territory (d) immediate future

Check your answers against the correct ones given below. The answers are not in order; this is to prevent your eye from catching sight of the correct answers before you have had a chance to do the exercise on your own.

5d. 17c. 10d. 18b. 7a. 1b. 12d. 22d. 20b. 11a. 23a. 2a. 14a. 9d. 16d. 6d. 19d. 21c. 24b. 4b. 15a. 13b. 3b. 8a.

Look up in your dictionary all the words for which you gave incorrect answers. Only when you have done this should you go on to the next exercise.

EXERCISE 5B

Each word in Word List 5 is used several times in the sentences below to illustrate different meanings or usage. One of the sentences for each word uses the italicized word incorrectly. You are to circle the letter preceding that sentence.

1. (a) The film received three Academy Awards, Hollywood's highest *accolade*. (b) Touching him on the shoulder with his sword, the king conferred the *accolade* of knighthood on the young man. (c) The people gathered in the streets to *accolade* the victorious army. (d) The *accolades* of the crowds meant little to the old actress.

2. (a) Joy is the *antipathy* of sorrow. (b) My feelings toward her can only be described as *antipathetic*. (c) His *antipathy* toward his native land is understandable since he was treated badly there. (d) An *antipathy* to soap and water is common in children.

3. (a) She wore a vivid red *carmine* draped across her shoulders. (b) The draperies were of rich velvet, dyed a deep *carmine*. (c) The sea glistened *carmine* in the setting sun.

4. (a) The neighboring towns and villages gradually *coalesced* into one sprawling city. (b) In 1854 a number of political parties *coalesced* to form the Republican Party. (c) Stars are formed by the *coalescence* of masses on interstellar dust. (d) The tar had *coalesced* to her coat, and nothing could remove it.

5. (a) Poker players and politicians must both learn to *dissimulate* for to show their true feelings can often be disastrous. (b) He tried to *dissimulate*, but his true feelings showed through. (c) They look the same, but actually they are quite *dissimulate*.

6. (a) Her *egotism* is monumental; every sentence begins with "I." (b) He is too *egotistical* to notice that he has no close friends. (c) It is completely *egotistical* which you choose, as they are both alike. (d) She is such an *egotist* that she is completely indifferent to the feelings of others.

7. (a) The doctor gave him some ointment to treat his skin *eruption*. (b) She *erupted* a back muscle while trying to move a heavy trunk. (c) Mount Vesuvius is an active volcano and can *erupt* at any time. (d) One moment he was sitting quietly, the next he had *erupted* into a violent rage.

8. (a) She handled the matter *felicitously* and with speed. (b) We were charmed by the *felicity* of her greeting. (c) With a house in the country and a stable of horses, his life was indeed *felicitous*. (d) They were charged with possessing a deadly weapon with *felicitous* intent.

9. (a) A rising *inflection* of the voice at the end of a sentence usually indicates a question. (b) The pronoun "he" can be *inflected* to form the possessive adjective "his." (c) Heavy losses were *inflected* on the enemy in yesterday's fighting.

10. (a) Each citizen has a duty to serve as a *jurist* when called. (b) Oliver Wendell Holmes (1841-1935), of the United States Supreme Court, was one of this country's greatest *jurists*. (c) Lord Coke, a seventeenth century English *jurist*, wrote many learned books on the law.

11. (a) The river begins to *meander* when it reaches the plain. (b) We *meandered* across the

town, looking idly in the store windows. (c) The kite string was so *meandered* that we could not unwind it from the spool. (d) The novel is a *meandering* account of a girl's growing up in the Midwest.

12. (a) The Internal Revenue Service was the *nemesis* that finally jailed Al Capone. (b) *Nemesis* pursued anyone defying the gods, or so the Greeks believed. (c) She threatened to *nemesis* anyone who disobeyed her. (d) After fleeing for many weeks, he finally turned and faced his *nemesis*.

13. (a) She tried to *novitiate* a number of improvements but met with little success. (b) The young *novitiates* were addressed by the abbot, who warned them of the rigors of monastic life. (c) The serious musician must undergo a long *novitiate* of practicing scales and octaves. (d) Before becoming a nun or a monk, a person must undergo a *novitiate* of at least one year.

14. (a) He refused to be seen driving last year's *outmoded* car style. (b) The manager's thinking is *outmoded*, and the board is thinking of replacing her. (c) The piston aircraft was quickly *outmoded* by the jet airliner. (d) They *outmoded* her into thinking it had been her own idea.

15. (a) The *protocol* was signed by all those present. (b) For many years he was chief of *protocol* in Washington. (c) The guests were arranged according to strict *protocol*, the ambassadors in front. (d) They looked very grand in the uniforms of *protocol* for the Prussian army.

16. (a) Her *specious* reasoning fooled us for a while since we had no reason to doubt its correctness. (b) They are not very bright and are easily misled by such *specious* arguments. (c) The judge rejected the claim because of its obvious *speciousness*. (d) The tall ceilings increase the *speciousness* of the room.

17. (a) James Whitcomb Riley wrote poetry in the *vernacular*. (b) They have a *vernacular* for picking up languages. (c) Sailors speak in a *vernacular* that is impossible for landlubbers to understand.

EXERCISE 5C

From the four numbered choices, complete the analogies below by underlining the word that stands in the same relationship to the third word as the second word does to the first. An explanation of analogies is given in the Introduction.

1. paint:brush::indite: (1) write (2) compose (3) pen (4) ink

2. visual:sight::tactile: (1) hear (2) touch (3) feel (4) sound

3. goldsmith:gold::lapidary: (1) gems (2) watches (3) silver (4) china

4. mace:authority::cornucopia: (1) horn (2) plenty (3) curved (4) hunger

5. freeze:frieze::sun: (1) warmth (2) moon (3) son (4) cold

6. primary:one::tertiary: (1) two (2) three (3) four (4) five

7. cold:warmth::insipid: (1) appetizing (2) heat (3) flavor (4) cold

8. inventory:stock::itinerary: (1) prices (2) route (3) list (4) destination

WORDLY WISE 5

A NOVITIATE is an inexperienced beginner, particularly in a religious order or, more generally, in any trade, career, or way of life. *Novice*, to some extent synonymous with *novitiate*, is a wider term and refers to a broader range of activities. A person may be a novice at playing the piano, but would be considered a novitiate only if planning to dedicate a considerable portion of his life to the art.

Etymology

Study the roots and prefixes given below together with the English words derived from them. Capitalized words are those given in the Word List. You should look up in a dictionary any words that are unfamiliar to you.

Prefixes: *e-* (out) Latin – Examples: *ERUPT, eject*
re- (again) Latin – Examples: *renovate, repair, reinstate*

Roots: *novus* (new) Latin – Examples: *NOVITIATE, novice, renovate*
rumpere (break) Latin – Examples: *ERUPT, rupture, interrupt*

Word List 6

AGENDA	EXACERBATE	OPPROBRIUM
APOPLECTIC	FEY	PRECIPITOUS
CIRCUMSPECT	INSATIABLE	REINSTATE
DENUDE	LAITY	THROES
DOTE	MORDANT	VICISSITUDES
EMOTE	NEUTER	

Look up the words above in your dictionary. Note that many of them have more than one meaning. When you feel that you know *all* the meanings of *all* the words, go on to the exercises below.

EXERCISE 6A

From the four choices following each phrase or sentence, you are to circle the letter preceding the one that is closest in meaning to the italicized word. Where the same word appears more than once, you should note that it is being used in different senses.

1. to prepare the *agenda* (a) brew supposed to have magical properties (b) route to be followed on a trip (c) substance taken to neutralize a poison (d) list of things to be done at a meeting

2. He was *apoplectic.* (a) suffering from temporary loss of memory (b) paralysed from a burst blood vessel in the brain (c) wasting away because of an inability to digest food (d) shortsighted

3. to be *circumspect* (a) vague (b) bold (c) cautious (d) round

4. to *denude* the land (a) put up for sale (b) make fertile (c) strip everything from (d) divide into tracts

5. to *dote* on someone (a) watch carefully over (b) be overly fond of (c) be highly critical of (d) have a strong aversion to

6. in her *dotage* (a) wise old age (b) prime of life (c) early youth (d) foolish old age

7. to watch someone *emote* (a) act without using words (b) attempt to conceal emotion (c) imitate the actions of another (d) express emotions dramatically

8. to *exacerbate* the situation (a) probe (b) ignore (c) improve (d) worsen

9. a *fey* manner (a) determined (b) playful (c) arrogant (d) oily

10. a *fey* warning (a) strongly worded (b) of impending death (c) lighthearted (d) unexpected

11. They were *insatiable.* (a) always wanting more (b) wantonly cruel (c) not up to standard (d) highly excited

12. a member of the *laity* (a) party attending a baby's baptism (b) military group apart from its officers (c) governing body of a church (d) religious group apart from its clergy

13. a *mordant* wit (a) foolish (b) gentle (c) biting (d) obscure

14. to use a *mordant* (a) chemical that bleaches away color (b) chemical that brings out a photographic image (c) chemical that makes metals rustproof (d) chemical that makes a dye permanent

15. a *neuter* creature (a) neither male nor female (b) of uncertain origin (c) able to change form (d) able to live on land or in water

16. to merit *opprobrium* (a) praise (b) disgrace (c) payment (d) ridicule

17. a *precipitous* slope (a) rocky (b) steep (c) smooth (d) wide

18. to *reinstate* someone (a) lend support to (b) remove from a position (c) appoint to a position of importance (d) restore to a former position.

19. the *throes* of death (a) warning signs (b) violent anguish (c) calm acceptance (d) eternal peace

20. after many *vicissitudes* (a) changes of fortune (b) harrowing experiences (c) false starts (d) stern warnings

Check your answers against the correct ones given below. The answers are not in order; this is to prevent your eye from catching sight of the correct answers before you have had a chance to do the exercise on your own.

12d. 3c. 15a. 8d. 17b. 16b. 18d. 2b. 11a. 4c. 10b. 14d. 13c. 5b. 20a. 7d. 1d. 6d. 19b. 9b.

Look up in your dictionary all the words for which you gave incorrect answers. Only when you have done this should you go on to the next exercise.

EXERCISE 6B

Each word in Word List 6 is used several times in the following sentences to illustrate different meanings or usage. One of the sentences for each word uses the italicized word incorrectly. You are to circle the letter preceding that sentence.

1. (a) The next item on the *agenda* is the appointment of a new secretary. (b) The *agenda* was prepared last week and cannot be changed just before the meeting. (c) She was chief *agenda* to the president for several years. (d) Following the fall of France, the next item on Hitler's *agenda* was the invasion of Russia.

2. (a) She is an *apoplectic* and believes she can foretell the future by reading cards. (b) He fell to the floor in an *apoplectic* fit. (c) The woman's condition was diagnosed as *apoplexy*, and she was rushed to the hospital. (d) He was almost *apoplectic* with rage.

3. (a) Ferdinand Magellan was killed in 1521 while *circumspecting* the earth. (b) She should be more *circumspect* in choosing how she will invest her money. (c) The investigation was carried out very *circumspectly*, and no one's feelings were hurt.

4. (a) They *denuded* the bark from the logs before splitting them. (b) The gallery had been *denuded* of all its paintings and looked strangely bare. (c) The once heavily-wooded grounds had been *denuded* of everything but a few shrubs.

5. (a) They *dote* on the two children and are always giving them gifts. (b) The old man must be in his *dotage* to have done such a silly thing. (c) He felt a great *dote* for his faithful old dog. (d) The parents looked *dotingly* upon their children, even though they treated the parents unkindly.

6. (a) It's fun to watch the old-time Hollywood actors *emote* in silent movies. (b) He *emoted* his lines so softly that we could hardly hear him from the first row. (c) That actress needs to show more restraint; she *emotes* far too much.

7. (a) His attempts to soothe her only *exacerbated* her rage. (b) "It serves you right," he *exacerbated*, delighting in her suffering. (c) Her condition was *exacerbated* by the improper treatment she received. (d) Ironically, by eliminating disease, we *exacerbate* the problem of feeding the world's hungry.

8. (a) A *fey* smile crossed her face, giving her an elfin, unworldly look. (b) Oberon, the king of the *feys,* took the hand of his fairy queen Titania. (c) Sir Walter Scott writes of a girl who was *fey* and therefore had not long to live.

9. (a) The children have an *insatiable* thirst for knowledge. (b) The problem is *insatiable* because there are too many unknown factors. (c) The more they paid the blackmailer, the more *insatiable* were the demands.

10. (a) She was made a *laity* and was able to perform various ceremonies of the church. (b) The cardinal urged all Catholics, both clergy and *laity*, to make greater efforts. (c) He was for many years a church layman, but he left the *laity* to become an ordained priest.

11. (a) She has a *mordant,* almost savage wit. (b) A metallic salt or other *mordant* is used to fix the dye permanently. (c) The soil had grown *mordant* with neglect, and nothing would grow on it. (d) The *mordancy* of the critic's review made the actors wince.

12. (a) "It" is a *neuter* pronoun. (b) Switzerland remained *neuter* during both world wars. (c) The amoeba, a *neuter* creature that lacks sex organs, multiplies by dividing.

13. (a) No *opprobrium* is attached to coming in last. (b) The tightrope walker held a long pole to maintain her *opprobrium*. (c) So *opprobrious* was her conduct that she was shunned by all who knew her. (d) The *opprobrium* that surrounds the name Benedict Arnold is fully deserved.

14. (a) He acted *precipitously* in giving them the money without checking their credentials. (b) It was damp and *precipitous* that morning, and rain had been predicted for later in the day.

15. (a) When it was realized she had been unjustly fired, she was immediately *reinstated*. (b) He *reinstated* as firmly as he knew how that no one would be allowed to leave. (c) Her *reinstatement* to the status of amateur after briefly playing as a professional is being challenged. (d) Everyone was delighted when he was *reinstated* as world champion.

16. (a) With a violent *throe* of her arms, she managed to free herself from her bonds. (b) They were young and in the *throes* of love and blind to everything else. (c) As we looked at the old man suffering, we knew he was in his death *throes*. (d) The country is currently in the *throes* of revolution.

17. (a) A strong faith may enable some people to cope with the *vicissitudes* of life. (b) Their soft lives had turned them into *vicissitudes*, unable to cope with life's ups and downs. (c) The *vicissitudes* of Christopher Columbus's voyages would have felled a lesser man.

EXERCISE 6C

This exercise is divided into two parts: Part A deals with synonyms, Part B with antonyms (these terms are explained in the Introduction). Allow fifteen minutes only for this test. If you cannot answer a question, go on to the next one without delay. If you have time left over at the end, go back and try to fill in unanswered questions.

26 or over correct:	excellent
22 to 25 correct:	good
21 or under correct:	thorough review of A exercises indicated

Part A (Synonyms)

Underline the word which is most *similar in meaning* to the capitalized word.

1. ARGUMENTATIVE
   iridescent   anomalous   abortive   captious precipitous

2. UNCHANGING
   svelte   equable   circumspect   insatiable disjointed

3. AWARD
   accolade frieze firmament rostrum coadjutor

4. PLAYFUL
   anomalous felicitous apoplectic fey insipid

5. CUSTOMS
   paroles mores throes norms liens

6. RICH
   captious insatiable opulent svelte specious

7. SAUNTER
   inflect emote educe meander dote

8. RED
   fey iridescent carmine protocol lapidary

9. STEEP
   outmoded apoplectic paregoric cosmic precipitous

10. BITING
    neuter mordant disjointed tertiary itinerary

11. ASSISTANT
    coadjutor maxim tocsin phalanx maestro

12. RESTORE
    inflect macerate reinstate educe foment

13. WRITE
    indite defray emote devolve desist

14. STANDARD
    neuter nemesis norm maxim motif

15. HONESTY
    empathy firmament vernacular tribulation probity

Part B (Antonyms)
Underline the word which is most nearly *opposite in meaning* to the capitalized word.

16. SEPARATE
    coalesce accolade dissimulate inflect oscillate

17. UP-TO-DATE
    anomalous disjointed precipitous meretricious outmoded

18. LIKING
    empirical probity antipathy lien neuter

19. HONOR
    tocsin mores nemesis protocol opprobrium

20. IMPROVE
    educe exacerbate emote exhume meander

21. CARELESS
    effete captious iridescent circumspect specious

22. OPEN
    clandestine mordant felicitous carmine foment

23. SUCCESSFUL
    paregoric abortive apoplectic mordant precipitous

24. BLAME
    coalesce educe exculpate infraction reinstate

25. STRONG
    refractory insipid insatiable effete disconsolate

26. PERMANENT
    evanescent tertiary emeritus collateral svelte

27. REGULAR
    dissimulate empirical lapidary anomalous mordant

28. TASTY
    trenchant itinerary insipid vibrant evanescent

29. TRACTABLE
    meretricious trenchant opulent refractory equable

30. INAPPROPRIATE
    felicitous disjointed circumspect specious refractory

Don't confuse FEY, which means "playful; in an elfin manner" and also "having to do with impending death," with *fay*, which is a poetic term and means "fairy."

A *layman* is a member of a church who does not belong to the clergy; the term is also used to describe a person not belonging to a particular profession (the doctor explained what was wrong in terms that a layman could understand). The plural of *layman* is *laymen*, but laymen taken collectively are referred to as the LAITY. (A minister is assisted by the laymen in his church. The bishop will give his annual address to the *laity* next Sunday.)

Note that THROES is seldom used in its singular form (an animal in its death throes; in the throes of violent change).

Etymology

Study the roots and prefix given below together with the English words derived from them. Capitalized words are those given in the Word List. You should look up in a dictionary any words that are unfamiliar to you.

Prefix: *circum-* (around) Latin — Examples: *CIRCUMSPECT*, *circum*ference, *circum*vent

Roots: *spectare* (to look) Latin — Examples: *CIRCUMSPECT*, retro*spect*, *spect*ator

acer (sharp) Latin — Examples: EX*ACER*BATE, *acer*bity

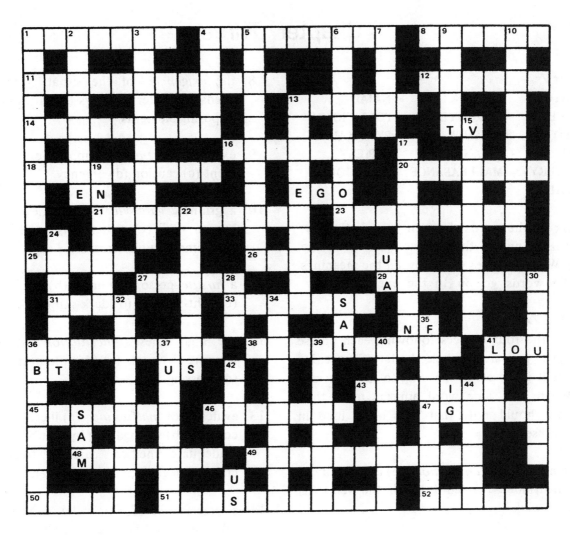

ACROSS

1. an agent of revenge or retribution
4. based on experience or experiment
8. to make bare; to strip
11. changes of fortune
12. an expert on law; a judge
13. to set down in writing (3)
14. depravity of conduct; vileness
16. the condition or amount most favorable
18. strong dislike
20. radiantly healthy (2)
21. charmingly appropriate
23. to restore to a position
25. customs; ways of doing things
26. seemingly true but actually false
27. a recurring element or theme (3)
29. a mark of achievement; an award
31. to show a foolish fondness for
33. having too high an opinion of oneself
36. abnormal; irregular
38. paralyzed because of a burst blood vessel in the brain
43. vivid red
45. a platform for speechmaking
46. honesty and uprightness
47. a list of things to be done, as at a meeting
48. to wind back and forth
49. cautious in what one says or does
50. to show emotion in a dramatic way
51. to conceal one's true feelings
52. violent anguish

DOWN

1. a novice in a religious order; a beginner
2. to soften by soaking in a liquid
3. always wanting more; unsatisfied
4. to arrive at by reasoning; to elicit
5. very steep
6. a fellow worker, especially one who assists
7. the members of a religion not belonging to the clergy
9. to burst forth
10. not connected; incoherent
13. showing changing rainbow colors
15. the everyday language of the common people
17. lasting but a short time; fleeting (3)
19. to change the pitch of the voice
22. unduly critical
24. sharply worded; biting
28. playful; in an elfin manner
30. to free from blame; to exonerate
32. to make worse; to exaggerate
34. public disgrace; shame
35. the dome of the sky; the heavens
36. unsuccessful; fruitless
37. no longer in style; outdated
39. diplomatic etiquette
40. to come together; to combine
41. a legal claim on the property of a debtor (3)
42. a rule or standard based on an average for the group
44. being neither masculine nor feminine

Chapter Three

Word List 7

AMBULATORY	EXIGENCIES	NAIAD
CIRCUMVENT	GARGOYLE	PONTIFICATE
CUCKOLD	HIRSUTE	PYROMANIAC
DIDACTIC	INCANTATION	SAPIENT
EFFRONTERY	MALFEASANCE	TECHNIQUE
ETHEREAL		

Look up the words above in your dictionary. Note that many of them have more than one meaning. When you feel you know *all* the meanings of *all* the words go on to the exercise below.

EXERCISE 7A

From the four choices following each phrase or sentence, you are to circle the letter preceding the one that is closest in meaning to the italicized word. Where the same word appears more than once, you should note that it is being used in different senses.

1. patients who are *ambulatory* (a) chronically ill (b) bedridden (c) fed through the veins (d) able to walk

2. to *circumvent* the enemy (a) meet head on (b) outwit (c) imitate (d) sign a treaty with

3. He is a *cuckold*. (a) old man with a very young wife (b) man who has been deserted by his wife (c) man whose wife is unfaithful (d) oft-married man

4. a *didactic* play (a) that amuses us (b) that bores us (c) that terrifies us (d) that instructs us

5. Such *effrontery*! (a) beauty (b) intelligence (c) impudence (d) courage

6. *ethereal* beauty (a) exotic (b) coarse (c) flawed (d) delicate

7. *ethereal* forms (a) invisible (b) present everywhere (c) light and airy (d) firm and solid

8. the *exigencies* of the situation (a) pressing needs (b) differing views (c) various causes (d) opposing elements

9. extreme *exigency* (a) opposition (b) disagreement (c) caution (d) urgency

10. a grinning *gargoyle* (a) mischievous girl (b) human skull (c) grotesquely carved figure (d) small, monkeylike creature

11. a *hirsute* person (a) hairy (b) smooth-skinned (c) light-skinned (d) dark-skinned

12. the high priest's *incantation* (a) words of warning (b) curse (c) formula of magic words (d) blessing

13. evidence of *malfeasance* (a) illegal entry into a country (b) wrongdoing by a public official (c) inadequate medical care or treatment (d) criminal neglect of one's children

14. a graceful *naiad* (a) ballet dancer (b) exit (c) dance step (d) water nymph

15. to *pontificate* (a) speak in a pompous manner (b) preside at a public meeting (c) think deeply (d) bring opposing factions together

16. He is a *pyromaniac*. (a) person with a compusion to eat (b) person with a fear of heights (c) person with a fear of enclosed spaces (d) person with a compulsion to start fires

17. a *sapient* observation (a) wise (b) foolish (c) cheerful (d) false

18. a revolutionary *technique* (a) discovery (b) method (c) material (d) theory

Check your answers against the correct ones given on the next page. The answers are not in order; this is to prevent your eye from catching sight of the correct answers before you have had a chance to do the exercise on your own.

9d. 1d. 15a. 2b. 10c. 6d. 8a. 5c. 11a. 3c. 17a. 12c. 4d. 14d. 7c. 18b. 13b. 16d.

Look up in your dictionary all the words for which you gave incorrect answers. Only when you have done this should you go on to the next exercise.

EXERCISE 7B

Each word in Word List 7 is used several times in the sentences below to illustrate different meanings or usage. One of the sentences for each word uses the italicized word incorrectly. You are to circle the letter preceding that sentence.

1. (a) *Ambulatory* patients will walk to the new wing; the others will be carried on stretchers. (b) These creatures are so primitive they have not yet reached the *ambulatory* stage in their evolution. (c) She was carried from the *ambulatory* into the hospital.

2. (a) She always finds a way to *circumvent* the schemes her enemies think up. (b) There are so many loopholes in this law that it is easy to *circumvent* it. (c) The authorities will search the ship thoroughly, but the refugee has ways of *circumventing* them. (d) She *circumvented* her rage on them by forbidding them to leave the house.

3. (a) The *cuckold* has the unpleasant habit of laying its eggs in other birds' nests. (b) When he discovered his wife had been unfaithful, he was afraid the whole town would know him for a *cuckold*. (c) She has been *cuckolding* him for years without his suspecting anything.

4. (a) To write a *didactic* play is to suppose the public is in need of your advice. (b) There are several *didactics* to the problem that have been overlooked. (c) The fables of Aesop, in addition to being enjoyable, are thoroughly *didactic*. (d) George Bernard Shaw thought of himself as a *didactic* writer.

5. (a) He had the *effrontery* to deny having taken part in the affair. (b) After she had lost my pen, she had the *effrontery* to ask for the loan of my pencil. (c) The two armies faced each other along a broad *effrontery*.

6. (a) Music so *ethereal* it seemed to come from heaven floated through the trees. (b) The bride, *ethereal* in white lace, floated down the aisle on the arm of her father. (c) He was *ethereal* with hunger when they rescued him.

7. (a) It is unfortunate that the *exigencies* of the present political situation prevent her attending the meeting. (b) In the *exigency* that they arrive late they can be seated at the back of the hall. (c) She must be prepared to cope with the *exigencies* of the moment while planning years into the future. (d) In this *exigency* the president must act without delay.

8. (a) The waterspouts from the roofs were often carved in the shape of grotesque *gargoyles*. (b) At each corner of the building was a hideous *gargoyle* carved out of stone. (c) He was terribly ugly, a *gargoyle* of a man. (d) She wore a woolen *gargoyle* draped loosely over her shoulders.

9. (a) Most of the male students were *hirsute* fellows, badly in need of haircuts. (b) She wore her hair in a neat *hirsute* fastened with a pin.

10. (a) Within seconds of drinking the *incantation*, he fell into a deep sleep. (b) The natives bowed their heads as the priest chanted the *incantation*. (c) The shaman's *incantation* was supposed to drive away evil spirits.

11. (a) The taking of bribes by a public official is a clear *malfeasance*. (b) They suspected the mayor of *malfeasance* although nothing was proved against her. (c) Despite the best medical care available, the *malfeasance* on his lung grew worse.

12. (a) You can cross the *naiad* further upstream where it becomes shallow. (b) The Greeks and Romans believed that lakes, rivers, and springs were inhabited by *naiads*.

13. (a) For an entire week newspaper editors *pontificated* on the secretary's resignation. (b) She particularly dislikes writers who *pontificate* on matters outside their field. (c) He *pontificated* deeply for a few moments before replying.

14. (a) Four barns had been burned down before the police caught the *pyromaniac* responsible. (b) Children who play with matches are not necessarily suffering from *pyromania.* (c) The sale of *pyromaniacs* such as rockets and sparklers is forbidden in this town.

15. (a) Her *sapience* is the result of decades of study and careful thought. (b) The *sapient* remarks of the judge made a strong impression on the jury. (c) The point you raise is interesting but is not *sapient* to what we are discussing.

16. (a) Painting in oils requires a different *technique* from watercolor work. (b) Workers are trained in the latest *techniques* of the industry. (c) The dancers worked hard, but their *technique* was often faulty. (d) The subject is too *technique* for us to go into here.

EXERCISE 7C

Complete the sentences below by filling in the appropriate form of either the word *connote* or the word *denote* (explanations of these terms are given in the Introduction).

1. We can tell what a word _____ by looking it up in a dictionary.

2. The same word may _____ quite different things to different people.

3. *Ice* _____ skating to many people who enjoy winter pastimes.

4. *Ice* _____ water reduced to its solid state by freezing.

5. The word *war* has unpleasant _____ to most people.

6. Five stars _____ the rank of General of the Army.

7. A word's _____ corresponds to its dictionary definition, but the _____ of a word are limitless.

8. The word *mother* _____ a female parent; it _____ love, warmth, and security.

WORDLY WISE 7

A GARGOYLE is a waterspout carved into a grotesque form projecting from the gutter of a building; such spouts are most frequently found on structures built during the medieval period. Etymologically, this word is related to *gargle* and *gurgle,* all three being derived from the Latin *gurgulio* (throat).

To PONTIFICATE is to speak dogmatically or pompously. Literally, since *pontiff* is another word for *pope,* it means to speak as though one possessed the authority of a pope.

Etymology

Study the roots given below together with the English words derived from them. Capitalized words are those given in the Word List. You should look up in a dictionary any words that are unfamiliar to you.

Roots: *sapere* (to be wise) Latin — Examples: SAP*I*ENT, Homo *sapi*ens

pyros (fire) Greek — Examples: *PYRO-MANIAC, pyre, pyro*technics

---

Word List 8

APOTHECARY	EXORCISE	PANEGYRIC
COLLOQUIAL	GENEALOGY	POTENTATE
CURATE	IMPECUNIOUS	RECANT
DISSEMBLE	LAVE	SCION
EPILOGUE	MERINO	TEMERITY
EVISCERATE		

Look up the words above in your dictionary. Note that many of them have more than one meaning. When you feel that you know *all* the meanings of *all* the words, go on to the following exercises.

EXERCISE 8A

From the four choices following each phrase or sentence, you are to circle the letter preceding the one that is closest in meaning to the italicized word. Where the same word appears more than once, you should note that it is being used in different senses.

1. an old *apothecary* (a) druggist (b) street vendor (c) soldier (d) wise person

2. *colloquial* expressions (a) mildly shocking (b) of formal writing (c) humorous (d) of everyday speech

3. a young *curate* (a) assistant to a surgeon (b) assistant to a senior officer (c) assistant to a rector or vicar (d) person in charge of a museum

4. to *dissemble* (a) take apart (b) pretend to be dead (c) become impatient (d) hide one's true feelings

5. a short *epilogue* (a) introductory speech in a play (b) speech spoken by a character to him- or herself (c) inscription on a tombstone (d) concluding speech in a play

6. to *eviscerate* an animal (a) perform experiments on (b) remove the entrails from (c) train (d) kill painlessly

7. to *exorcise* the ghost (a) be afraid of (b) drive out (c) receive messages from (d) perceive

8. an expert on *genealogy* (a) the study of ancient peoples (b) the study of primitive peoples (c) the study of family descent (d) the study of the effects of old age

9. to be *impecunious* (a) faultlessly attired (b) strict (c) lazy (d) without money

10. to *lave* the hands (a) wring (b) wash (c) bind (d) stroke

11. a fine *merino* (a) sheep with long, silky wool (b) dueling sword of Spanish steel (c) bull used for breeding purposes (d) shawl made of pure silk

12. to deliver a *panegyric* (a) ultimatum threatening war (b) complaint in a whining tone (c) formal speech of praise (d) formal message from a head of state

13. to meet the *potentate* (a) children's nurse (b) powerfully-built man (c) large ocean liner (d) powerful ruler

14. to *recant* (a) make a second attempt (b) entertain in a grand manner (c) publicly repudiate one's beliefs (d) keep happening

15. a twelve-year-old *scion* (a) child whose parents are dead (b) child of great intelligence (c) descendant (d) child who leaves home

16. a freshly-cut *scion* (a) root used for medicine (b) bud used for grafting (c) leaf used for smoking (d) flower used for perfume

17. to show *temerity* (a) rashness (b) fear (c) curiosity (d) anger

Check your answers against the correct ones given below. The answers are not in order; this is to prevent your eye from catching sight of the correct answers before you have had a chance to do the exercise on your own.

13d. 16b. 12c. 4d. 14c. 7b. 5d. 11a. 3c. 17a. 2d. 10b. 6b. 8c. 9d. 1a. 15c.

Look up in your dictionary all the words for which you gave incorrect answers. Only when you have done this should you go on to the next exercise.

EXERCISE 8B

Each word in Word List 8 is used several times in the following sentences to illustrate different meanings or usage. One of the sentences for each word uses the italicized word incorrectly. You are to circle the letter preceding that sentence.

1. (a) Many modern drugstores use *apothecary* jars as window decorations. (b) The druggist

mixed him an *apothecary* which he was to take before retiring to bed. (c) Drams, grains and scruples are measures of weight that *apothecaries* used in making up drugs. (d) The pharmacist is the modern counterpart of the *apothecary* of long ago.

2. (a) They dressed *colloquially* in sweaters, blue jeans, and loafers. (b) "My buddy flunked" is a *colloquial* way of saying, "My friend failed." (c) *Colloquial* expressions should be avoided in formal writing. (d) Their speech is full of "aint's," "dunnos," and other *colloquialisms*.

3. (a) The elderly minister was glad to have a young *curate* to help him. (b) The young *curate* looked forward to having a church of his own one day. (c) She was appointed *curate* of the town museum last year.

4. (a) She could *dissemble* the parts and put them back together without even looking. (b) It is sad that children, who are naturally truthful, should be taught to *dissemble*. (c) We often are *dissemblers*, saying one thing while believing another. (d) As it was useless to *dissemble*, she told them exactly how she felt about the idea.

5. (a) Several of Shakespeare's plays end with an *epilogue* in which one of the characters addresses the audience directly. (b) Lincoln's assassination was a sad *epilogue* to the Civil War. (c) Many of the tombstones had humorous *epilogues* carved on them.

6. (a) In rewriting the book, she has *eviscerated* it and made it a mere story for boys. (b) The meat had been left outside and was starting to *eviscerate*. (c) *Eviscerated* turkeys are on sale this week. (d) The hunters quickly *eviscerated* and skinned the deer.

7. (a) Sprinkling holy water about the house is supposed to *exorcise* ghosts. (b) They thought the ghost had been *exorcised*, but it returned the following night. (c) They liked to *exorcise* their wits by asking each other riddles. (d) Following the *exorcism* of the ghost, a short thanksgiving service was held.

8. (a) A person skilled in *genealogy* can trace your family back for many generations. (b) The *genealogy* of this disease is not known. (c) She has traced her *genealogy* back to the fifteenth century. (d) He is an amateur *genealogist* and has traced his family back for ten generations.

9. (a) She wore an *impecunious* dressing gown of gorgeous gold brocade. (b) The money is distributed to the *impecunious* families of the town. (c) Now that he is wealthy he loves to boast of his *impecunious* childhood. (d) They didn't have a penny but seemed not at all worried by their *impecuniousness*.

10. (a) Baptism is performed by *laving* the infant's head with holy water. (b) She *laved* her injured foot in a small stream. (c) The *lave* from the volcano hardens into pumice. (d) The island's beaches are *laved* by the warm Pacific waters.

11. (a) The sweater was made of the finest *merino* wool. (b) The *merino* produces fine silky wool, but its meat is not of high quality. (c) *Merino* is a cloth so fine it is barely distinguishable from cashmere. (d) She wore a *merino* made of the finest wool.

12. (a) He was modest enough to blush at the *panegyrics* of the various speakers. (b) She performed a few *panegyrics* to loosen up her muscles before the game. (c) The poem is really a *panegyric* to the poet's native land.

13. (a) The *potentates* of several eastern kingdoms are holding meetings this week. (b) He is one of the last Hollywood *potentates* to rule his studio single-handedly. (c) The poison is so *potentate* that a single drop can kill a person. (d) She rules, not as a *potentate* with absolute power, but as an elected official.

14. (a) Following their *recantations* in the court-room, the political prisoners were freed. (b) Galileo was forced to *recant* his belief that the earth revolves around the sun. (c) Joan of Arc was burned to death as a heretic because she would not *recant*. (d) The roof should be *recanted* slightly so that the rain can flow off.

15. (a) The *scions* of some of the state's wealthiest families attend this school. (b) The *scion* must be grafted to the plant at just the right time if it is to take. (c) She is very unassuming although she is the *scion* of one of the town's wealthiest families. (d) He is expected to *scion* a large fortune when his father dies.

16. (a) The *temerity* of the steel is increased by its being heated and allowed to cool slowly. (b) No one had the *temerity* to question the nurse's orders. (c) The workhouse master was speechless at the *temerity* of Oliver's asking for more.

EXERCISE 8C

In each of the sentences below a word is omitted. From the four words provided, select the one that best completes the sentence. Allow ten minutes for this test. If you cannot answer a question, go on to the next one without delay. If you have time left over at the end, go back and try to fill in unanswered questions.

18 or over correct:	excellent
14 to 17 correct:	good
13 or under correct:	thorough review of A exercises indicated

1. . . . . patients are encouraged to get out of bed and walk around.
   disjointed ethereal ambulatory anomalous

2. Her . . . . review of the play greatly upset the actors.
   iridescent tactile trenchant impecunious

3. As the speaker left the . . . ., a storm of applause broke out.
   rostrum mace accolade protocol

4. These minor political groups will probably . . . . into a single large party.
   circumvent dissemble novitiate coalesce

5. I must ask you to . . . . from questioning me.
   defray desist devolve indite

6. That young recruit had the . . . . to talk back to the sergeant.
   clandestine malfeasance temerity didactic

7. Their disgraceful conduct merits the . . . . heaped upon them.
   collateral nemesis malfeasance opprobrium

8. After several . . . . attempts, they gave up their efforts.
   abortive effete disconsolate mordant

9. Her . . . . circumstances forced her to live very frugally.
   sapient ethereal impecunious meretricious

10. Her . . . . rise to power stunned the entire nation.
    apoplectic trenchant meteoric empirical

11. The heretic refused to . . . . and was burned at the stake.
    exculpate exorcise recant defray

12. We must find a way to . . . . the enemy's plans.
    circumvent dissemble cuckold impeach

13. The people here speak in a . . . . that outsiders find hard to understand.
    didactic vernacular colloquial paregoric

14. Your attempts to help will only . . . . the situation.
    exacerbate exorcise macerate exculpate

15. . . . . requires that heads of state be received first.
    temerity genealogy protocol paregoric

16. Our . . . . includes a one-night stopover in Chicago.
panegyric accolade itinerary cornucopia

17. The . . . . made up a drug that he swore would cure the disease.
pyromaniac apothecary scion curate

18. He admired the . . . . beauty of the patch of oil on the water.
didactic anomalous empirical iridescent

19. Her . . . . wit made her a popular guest at dinner parties.
mordant ethereal hirsute specious

20. The river . . . . gently across the plain.
paroles emotes meanders laves

WORDLY WISE 8

A CURATE is a young member of the clergy assigned to assist a minister. A *curator* is a person who has charge of a museum, library, or similar institution. Do not confuse these two terms.

DISSEMBLE and *dissimulate* (Word List 5) both mean "to disguise one's true feelings or intentions," and no clear distinction can be made between the two terms.

A suffix meaning "the science or study of" is *-logy*. The vowel preceding this suffix is part of the root and most frequently, it is *o* as in *biology* (from *bios*, "life"). GENEALOGY, meaning "an account of the descent of a person or group" or the study of family pedigrees, is spelled with an *a* from the Greek root *genea* ("race," "family").

LAVE, meaning "wash," is a poetic term and is rarely used in everyday speech.

The *c* in SCION is silent; pronounce this word *SY-ən.*

Etymology

Study the roots and prefixes given above together with the English words derived from them. Capitalized words are those given in the Word List. You should look up in a dictionary any words that are unfamiliar to you.

Prefixes: *col-* (together) Latin – Examples: *COL-LOQUIAL, col*laborate, *col*lateral

im- (not) Latin – Examples: *IMPE-CUNIOUS, im*possible

Roots: *loquor* (speak) Latin – Examples: *COL-LOQUIAL, loqu*acious, *eloqu*ent

pecunia (money) Latin – Examples: *IM-PECUN*IOUS, *pecun*iary

---

Word List 9

CATHOLIC	HALCYON	PULSATE
CORRELATE	INANIMATE	REFERENDUM
DEDUCE	LUNAR	ROE
DURANCE	MISDEMEANOR	SYMPOSIUM
EQUIVOCAL	PARSON	VENIRE
EXCRESCENCE		

Look up the words above in your dictionary. Note that many of them have more than one meaning. When you feel you know *all* the meanings of *all* the words go on to the exercise below.

EXERCISE 9A

From the four choices following each phrase or sentence, you are to circle the letter preceding the one that is closest in meaning to the italicized word. Where the same word appears more than once, you should note that it is being used in different senses.

1. *catholic* tastes (a) conventional (b) broad in scope (c) of long standing (d) narrowly defined

2. the *Catholic* church (a) reformed (b) ancient (c) universal (d) orthodox

3. to *correlate* the results (a) question (b) go over (c) confirm (d) bring together

4. to *deduce* something (a) figure out (b) be suspicious of (c) decrease the amount of (d) have strong feelings concerning

5. *durance* vile (a) mockery (b) shame (c) imprisonment (d) death

6. an *equivocal* answer (a) direct (b) hesitant (c) complete (d) misleading

7. an *equivocal* result (a) doubtful (b) fair (c) final (d) prearranged

8. the cause of the *excrescence* (a) outgrowth (b) fracture (c) painful experience (d) failure of a vital part

9. *halcyon* days (a) troubled (b) slowly-passing (c) quickly-passing (d) peaceful

10. *inanimate* matter (a) lacking form (b) lacking stability (c) lacking life (d) lacking the ability to combine chemically

11. an *inanimate* style (a) well-disciplined (b) lively (c) undisciplined (d) dull

12. *lunar* observations (a) of the planets (b) of the stars (c) of the sun (d) of the moon

13. It is a *misdemeanor.* (a) warning (b) serious crime (c) minor crime (d) punishment

14. a kindly *parson* (a) stranger (b) children's nurse (c) clergyman (d) prison guard

15. to *pulsate* (a) sway (b) throb (c) stagger (d) increase

16. to hold a *referendum* (a) direct vote on a proposed law (b) mass meeting to protest a law (c) election to choose a party's candidate (d) examination to determine a person's suitability for office

17. to eat the *roe* (a) dried beef (b) cow's stomach (c) goose's liver (d) fish's eggs

18. a young *roe* (a) European rabbit (b) European bear (c) European deer (d) European squirrel

19. to hold a *symposium* (a) tryout for young musicians (b) all-night vigil over a dead body (c) final rehearsal for a play (d) conference for discussing some subject

20. to bring together the *venire* (a) opposing parties in a lawsuit (b) panel from which jurors are selected (c) facts that comprise the evidence in a trial (d) panel of judges in an appeals court

Check your answers against the correct ones given below. The answers are not in order; this is to prevent your eye from catching sight of the correct answers before you have had a chance to do the exercise on your own.

9d. 1b. 15b. 19d. 2c. 10c. 6d. 8a. 5c. 11d. 3d. 17d. 12d. 4a. 14c. 7a. 18c. 20b. 13c. 16a.

Look up in your dictionary all the words for which you gave incorrect answers. Only when you have done this should you go on to the next exercise.

EXERCISE 9B

Each word in Word List 9 is used several times in the sentences below to illustrate different meanings or usage. One of the sentences for each word uses the italicized word incorrectly. You are to circle the letter preceding that sentence.

1. (a) The *catholicity* of the children's reading habits surprised me. (b) Before the Reformation *Catholicism* was the single and universal religion of most of Europe. (c) The librarian is a man of *catholic* tastes who enjoys a detective story as much as he does German philosophy. (d) It is a *catholic* law of nature that matter cannot be created or destroyed.

2. (a) There seems to be a high *correlation* between ignorance and prejudice. (b) There is no better *correlative* for a headache than the simple aspirin. (c) The results of the experiments must be *correlated* before any conclusions are drawn. (d) The *correlative* conjunctions are "either" and "or" and "neither" and "nor."

3. (a) The existence of the planet Neptune was *deduced* from the behavior of the other planets. (b) Charitable gifts may be *deduced*

from one's earnings in figuring out one's taxes. (c) The answer is easily *deducible* from the facts given. (d) The detective, after cogitating for a few moments, made the brilliant *deduction* that the butler had committed the murder.

4. (a) The art treasures were shipped to the country for the *durance* of the war. (b) After suffering *durance* vile for many long years, the prisoner was finally released. (c) The prisoner had undergone *durance* and torture, but he still refused to confess.

5. (a) Results of the experiment were *equivocal* and indicated that more experimentation is needed. (b) A liter is approximately *equivocal* to one quart. (c) Her *equivocal* answers showed clearly that she had something to hide. (d) "Do not *equivocate*," said the principal. "Answer the question in a direct and straightforward manner."

6. (a) Warts are abnormal *excrescences* from the skin. (b) The house would look quite modern if the Victorian *excrescences* were stripped away. (c) They shouted violent *excrescences* at us for breaking their window. (d) Hair is a normal *excrescence* from the scalp.

7. (a) His mind went back to the *halcyon* days of his youth that he had spent on his grandmother's farm. (b) The poet Shelley speaks of "the brightest hour of unborn spring . . . the *halcyon* morn." (c) She's usually ill-natured when she gets out of bed, but this morning she seems quite *halcyon*. (d) The King Arthur legends take us back to the *halcyon* age of Camelot.

8. (a) The *inanimate* and uninventive dance routines brought only yawns from the audience. (b) A single blow from his fist could make a person *inanimate*. (c) Science has created what appears to be life from *inanimate* matter.

9. (a) Pictures of the *lunar* landscape can be transmitted to earth by television. (b) A *lunar* month, the period from new moon to new moon, lasts 29 1/2 days. (c) A *lunar* eclipse occurs when the moon is obscured by the earth's shadow. (d) The *lunars* of the moon are caused by its position relative to the sun.

10. (a) Driving without a license is a *misdemeanor* punishable by a fine of fifty dollars. (b) You *misdemeanor* yourself by associating with such undesirables. (c) A person can be sent to the penitentiary for a felony but not for a *misdemeanor*.

11. (a) He was the *parson* of the village church for over forty years. (b) The congregation planned to redecorate the *parsonage* for the new minister. (c) The minister agreed to *parson* all those who truly repented of their sins.

12. (a) She could feel the *pulsating* of her heart. (b) The *pulsations* of the engine increased until the whole plane was vibrating. (c) She *pulsated* her foot on the floor in time to the music. (d) The whole town was *pulsating* with life.

13. (a) The *referendum* requires a two-thirds majority vote to pass. (b) A *referendum* will be held to determine if taxes should be raised to pay for the new school. (c) We will take the intersection of the two lines as our *referendum* point.

14. (a) The *roe* is a small, graceful deer found in Europe and Asia. (b) The *roe's* eggs are a highly-prized delicacy in certain parts of the world. (c) Caviar is the salted *roe* of the sturgeon or other large fish. (d) A *roe*buck and its hind were standing in the forest clearing.

15. (a) It is impossible for a person to attend all the *symposia* that are being held. (b) The role of industry in town planning will be the subject of today's *symposium*. (c) A number of *symposiums* are being held during College Week. (d) It was the *symposium* of the meeting that we support the proposals.

16. (a) She was filled with *venire* when she saw she had been tricked. (b) From the *venire*, twelve jury members will be selected. (c) The *venire*men assembled in the courtroom for questioning by lawyers of both sides.

EXERCISE 9C

This exercise combines synonyms and antonyms. You are to underline the word which is *either* most similar in meaning *or* most nearly opposite in meaning to the capitalized word. Underline only one word for each question after deciding that it is either an antonym or a synonym and write *A* (for antonym) or *S* (for synonym) after the capitalized word. Allow 15 minutes only for this test. If you cannot answer a question, go on to the next one without delay. If you have time left over at the end, go back and try to fill in unanswered questions.

26 or over correct: excellent
22 to 25 correct: good
21 or under correct: thorough review of A exercises indicated

1. LIVELY . . . .
tertiary lapidary meretricious inanimate apoplectic

2. UNIVERSAL . . . .
catholic collateral emeritus optimum carmine

3. CLUMSY . . . .
felicitous opulent disconsolate specious anomalous

4. OUTWIT . . . .
devolve ensemble circumvent dote educe

5. URGENCY . . . .
probity potentate itinerary tribulation exigency

6. WEALTHY . . . .
equable vibrant impecunious sapient ethereal

7. SWIFT . . . .
didactic equivocal meteoric felicitous specious

8. AWARD . . . .
accolade phalanx scion emeritus halcyon

9. EXPEL . . . .
exhume temporize exorcise correlate meander

10. SOLID . . . .
phalanx ethereal effeminate impecunious equivocal

11. FLEETING . . . .
inanimate lapidary tertiary vernacular evanescent

12. TURBULENT . . . .
cosmic hirsute tactile colloquial halcyon

13. GENTLE . . . .
disconsolate mordant anomalous rheumy curate

14. VILIFICATION . . . .
palfrey cornucopia panegyric referendum naiad

15. OUTGROWTH . . . .
epilogue maxim excrescence tocsin norm

16. FOOLHARDY . . . .
circumspect meretricious firmament colloquial cuckold

17. DIRECT . . . .
collateral sapient refractory novitiate equivocal

18. WASH . . . .
exorcise parole lave erupt fey

19. SMOOTH-FACED . . . .
effete tactile fey hirsute halcyon

20. DRUGGIST . . . .
trajectory refractory apothecary novitiate pyromaniac

21. VIGOROUS . . . .
lien correlate devolve pontificate effete

22. INFER . . . .

defray deduce eviscerate reinstate desist

23. INSTRUCTIVE . . . .

potentate clandestine paregoric didactic
abortive

24. REPUDIATE . . . .

recant parole deduce devolve inflect

25. THROB . . . .

asphyxiate pulsate vibrant exculpate macerate

26. IMPROVE . . . .

educe temporize circumvent exacerbate
foment

27. FOOLISH . . . .

sapient anomalous ensemble iridescent lunar

28. IMPRISONMENT . . . .

durance trajectory itinerary parole throes

29. METHOD . . . .

phalanx venire durance itinerary technique

30. CAUTION . . . .

carmine temerity ensemble agenda durance

WORDLY WISE 9

CATHOLIC, when spelled with a small *c*,
means "universal, broad in scope" (a person of
catholic tastes); when spelled with a capital *c*, it
refers to the Church of Rome as opposed to the
Protestant Church. It should be noted that the
Catholic Church, prior to the Reformation, was the
universal church of Europe.

DEDUCE means "infer," and a deduction is
something deduced or inferred. Note that *deduction* also means "something subtracted" (I deduced that the $30 deduction from my paycheck
was for income tax, and my deduction was
correct).

DURANCE, meaning "imprisonment," is an
archaic term that survives chiefly in the phrase "in
durance vile," a phrase considered by many to be a
cliche.

A MISDEMEANOR is a minor offense, one
not punishable by death or by imprisonment in a
state penitentiary. A *felony* is a serious crime,
punishment of which may take either of the above
forms.

The plural of SYMPOSIUM is *symposia* or
symposiums.

Etymology

Study the roots and prefix given below together with the English words derived from them.
Capitalized words are those given in the Word List.
You should look up in a dictionary any words that
are unfamiliar to you.

Prefix: *sym-* (together) Greek — Examples:
*sym*pathy, SY*M*POSIUM

Roots: *posis* (drinking) Greek — Example:
SYM*POSIS*UM

aequus (same, even) Latin — Examples:
*EQU*IVOCAL, *equ*able, *equ*itable

vox, voc (voice) Latin — Examples: EQUIV-
OCAL, *voc*al, *voc*iferous

ACROSS

1. to drive out (evil spirits) by incantation
5. to hide one's true feelings
9. to throb; to vibrate
11. without money
14. a Protestant minister
16. universal; all-inclusive
17. pressing needs
18. the eggs of a fish
19. intended to instruct or inform
22. foolish or reckless boldness
23. imprisonment; physical restraint
25. the path of an object fired into the air (2)
27. to wash
28. to publicly repudiate one's beliefs
29. light and airy; delicate
30. a sheep with long, silky wool
34. a person with a compulsion to start fires
36. to remove everything from; to strip (6)
38. a method of working or doing something
41. a panel from which jurors are selected
42. without life
43. a shameless boldness
45. an assistant to a member of the clergy
46. an offspring, especially of wealthy or
    important parents
47. able to walk
48. stone waterspout carved into a grotesque shape
49. a normal or abnormal outgrowth
50. a conference for discussing some subject

DOWN

1. to remove the entrails from
2. a man whose wife is unfaithful to him
3. wealthy; very rich (1)
4. wrongdoing in public affairs
5. to figure out by reasoning
6. full of knowledge; wise
7. a minor crime
8. of, like, or relating to the moon
10. a formal speech of praise
12. a powerful ruler; a monarch
13. a water nymph
15. to prevent (or get the better of) by trickery
20. chanted words believed to have magical properties
21. to bring together in relation with one another
24. of or relating to everyday speech
26. to speak pompously and with undue self-assurance
31. deliberately ambiguous
32. one who makes up and sells drugs
33. the submission of a law to a direct vote of the people
35. the study of family descent
37. a concluding speech in a play
39. covered with hair; hairy
40. calm; peaceful
44. to show emotion in a very dramatic way (6)

Chapter Four

Word List 10

ACCOUTER	INVEIGLE	PERORATION
AXIOM	LARVA	SACRILEGE
BEREFT	MAGNILOQUENT	SUFFUSE
CORTEGE	MASTICATE	UNIMPEACHABLE
DISDAIN	NIRVANA	VERDANT
GRATUITOUS	OCTAVO	

Look up the words above in your dictionary. Note that many of them have more than one meaning. When you feel you know *all* the meanings of *all* the words, go on to the exercise below.

EXERCISE 10A

From the four choices following each phrase or sentence, you are to circle the letter preceding the one that is closest in meaning to the italicized word. Where the same word appears more than once, you should note that it is being used in different senses.

1. to *accouter* the men (a) equip (b) recognize (c) greet (d) outwit

2. to learn the *axiom* (a) true identity (b) self-evident truth (c) answer to a trick question (d) chemical formula

3. *bereft* of power (a) full (b) ignorant (c) deprived (d) careless

4. They were *bereft*. (a) heartened by good news (b) left lonely by some loss (c) left money under a will (d) sympathetic to the needs of others

5. a monarch's *cortege* (a) marriage partner (b) ceremonial gown (c) royal funeral (d) train of attendants

6. a funeral *cortege* (a) procession of mourners (b) graveside service (c) carriage bearing the coffin (d) hymn of farewell

7. a look of *disdain* (a) fear (b) scorn (c) determination (d) anger

8. *gratuitous* lessons (a) free (b) expensive (c) regular (d) difficult

9. a *gratuitous* insult (a) sly (b) deserved (c) open (d) uncalled for

10. to *inveigle* someone (a) lure (b) invite (c) honor (d) delight

11. to study the *larva* (a) hot, melted rock from a volcano (b) tiny, one-celled animalcule (c) insect in its earliest stage after hatching (d) hard substance made of the skeletons of tiny sea creatures

12. a *magniloquent* speech (a) piously religious (b) smoothly delivered (c) pompously boastful (d) intensely patriotic

13. to *masticate* food (a) season (b) chew (c) cook (d) overindulge in

14. to attain *nirvana* (a) an abundance of material possessions (b) a state of peace among nations (c) a state of perfect blessedness (d) resistance to disease

15. printed on *octavo* (a) a page-size 18 inches by 11½ inches (b) a page-size 11½ inches by 9 inches (c) a page-size 6 inches by 9 inches (d) a page-size 6 inches by 4½ inches

16. a moving *peroration* (a) introduction to an epic poem (b) plea for mercy (c) hymn of praise (d) final part of a speech

17. an act of *sacrilege* (a) respect for what is sacred (b) atonement for one's sins (c) disrespect for what is sacred (d) supreme self-sacrifice

18. to *suffuse* something (a) inject into (b) take apart (c) render harmless (d) spread over

19. *unimpeachable* conduct (a) surreptitious (b) blameless (c) indescribable (d) blameworthy

20. *verdant* grass (a) green (b) parched (c) waving (d) long

Check you answers against the correct ones given below. The answers are not in order; this is to prevent your eye from catching sight of the correct answers before you have had a chance to do the exercise on your own.

9d. 2b. 5d. 12c. 18d. 20a. 4b. 11c. 10a. 1a. 15c. 6a. 3c. 14c. 13b. 16d. 7b. 17c. 8a. 19b.

Look up in your dictionary all the words for which you gave incorrect answers. Only when you have done this should you go on to the next exercise.

EXERCISE 10B

Each word in Word List 10 is used several times in the sentences below to illustrate different meanings or usage. One of the sentences for each word uses the italicized word incorrectly. You are to circle the letter preceding that sentence.

1. (a) The hikers were *accoutered* for stormy weather in boots and rubber coats. (b) Rifles, field guns, field packs, and other *accouterments* of war littered the roadside. (c) The soldier adjusted his *accouter* and fell into line with the others.

2. (a) Students are required to learn the *axioms* of Euclidean geometry. (b) It is an *axiom* of business practice that specialization increases efficiency. (c) That the part is less than the whole is *axiomatic*. (d) The line cuts the *axiom* of the triangle into two equal parts.

3. (a) Under the terms of the will, she was *bereft* five thousand dollars a year. (b) The speaker was a sad-faced individual, totally *bereft* of humor. (c) *Bereft* of hope, the prisoner sat dejected in his tiny prison cell.

4. (a) The *cortege*, consisting of five hundred mourners, made its way to the cemetery. (b) The *cortege* was ceremoniously unfolded and placed over the coffin. (c) The king and his *cortege* entered the palace to a fanfare of trumpets.

5. (a) She treated his offer with the *disdain* it deserved. (b) They looked *disdainfully* at the boy who had made the suggestion. (c) She *disdained* the job as being beneath her dignity. (d) I am *disdained* that you have taken such unfair advantage of them.

6. (a) The services performed by our group are entirely *gratuitous* so don't worry. (b) I am extremely *gratuitous* of all that you have done for me. (c) You *gratuitously* assumed that I would have no further need of it, but you are mistaken. (d) Before I could say a word, he began hurling *gratuitous* insults at me.

7. (a) He hoped to *inveigle* her into marrying him. (b) Don't let them *inveigle* you into doing something you know is wrong. (c) She tried every *inveigle* she could think of to lure him into proposing.

8. (a) Hot molten *larva* poured down the sides of the erupting volcano. (b) A caterpillar is the *larva* of a butterfly. (c) An insect, emerging from the egg, becomes first a *larva*, then a pupa, finally a fully-developed insect.

9. (a) The *magniloquent* self-praise of the speaker was too much for us and we left. (b) She was a small-town country lawyer who mistook *magniloquence* for eloquence. (c) The building, with its long row of marble columns, was truly *magniloquent*.

10. (a) Since most of her teeth are missing, she finds it hard to *masticate* properly. (b) The machine *masticates* the wood chips into a smooth paste. (c) *Mastication* is always a little uncomfortable when one is wearing newly-fitted dentures. (d) They *masticated* the problem carefully before coming to a decision.

11. (a) The priest intoned the words of the *nirvana* to the band of worshipers. (b) Buddhists believe that when the self becomes part of the supreme spirit, *nirvana* is attained. (c) *Nirvana* is the triumphing over the desires, the hatreds, even the awareness of the individual self.

12. (a) A book-size with eight pages cut from a sheet is called *octavo*. (b) A quarto book-size is twice as large as an *octavo* and half the size of a folio. (c) The most common book-size is *octavo*, measuring approximately six inches by nine inches. (d) A beginning pianist must practice *octavos* over and over.

13. (a) She concluded with a fine *peroration* in which she thanked the people for their support. (b) He sang a number of drinking songs, with the crowd joining in the *peroration* of each one. (c) She is working on her speech but is having some difficulty with the *peroration*.

14. (a) The raiders broke into churches and committed numerous acts of *sacrilege*. (b) The nobles who murdered Thomas á Becket inside Canterbury Cathedral were guilty of *sacrilege*. (c) The stealing of the candles from the altar was a *sacrilegious* act. (d) The burial was conducted according to the holy *sacrileges* of the church.

15. (a) A blush *suffused* his cheeks when we asked the name of his girl friend. (b) She was *suffused* in her apologies for keeping us waiting.(c) A vivid red glow *suffused* the western sky as the sun sank below the horizon.

16. (a) Apart from a few minor *unimpeachables*, he has led a blameless life. (b) My information was obtained from *unimpeachable* sources. (c) She has an *unimpeachable* reputation in business.

17. (a) His eyes swept proudly over the acres of *verdant* farmland. (b) *Verdant* grew in profusion on the slopes of the coastal hills. (c) The *verdancy* of the meadows is due to the heavy spring rains.

EXERCISE 10C

phil(o) (lover of)	*ataleie* (tax exempt)
mis(o) (hater of)	*gyne* (woman)
anthropos (man)	*sophos* (wise)
logos (word; study of)	*eidos* (shape)

Using the above Greek roots separately or in combination, construct words to match the definitions below.

1. _____ the study of the health and treatment of disease in women

2. _____ the collection and study of postage stamps

3. _____ one who has an intense dislike for mankind

4. _____ one who is deeply interested in words and their origins

5. _____ of or relating to the most highly-developed and manlike apes

6. _____ a person who loves and pursues wisdom

7. _____ the study of the races, customs, characteristics, etc. of mankind

8. _____ one with an intense dislike for women

9. _____ the desire to help mankind, as shown by charitable acts

WORDLY WISE 10

BEREFT and *bereaved* are past participles of the verb *bereave*. Both refer to one who has suffered a loss, but note that *bereaved* suggests a loss of a person (a bereaved family mourning a death in the family), while *bereft* suggests a different kind of loss (bereft of hope).

Size designations commonly used in the book trade today were originally based on a sheet of paper measuring nineteen by twenty-four inches.

An OCTAVO book was one with pages cut eight from a printing sheet and thus measured approximately six inches by nine inches; *octavo* is commonly abbreviated *8vo*. A book with pages cut four from a page and twice as large was called a *quarto*. The largest book size is *folio*, made by folding the printing sheet into two pages.

PERORATION, technically speaking, refers to the closing part of a formal speech; more generally, it is used to refer to the speech in its entirety.

Word List 11

AFFINITY	INTERCEDE	PLETHORA
BACCHANALIAN	LINGUIST	SMELT
BLASPHEMOUS	MALAPROPISM	SURROGATE
DECENNIAL	MAUDLIN	UPBRAID
EXPATIATE	NUGATORY	VOCAL
HOMOGENEOUS	PANTHEON	

Look up the words above in your dictionary. Note that many of them have more than one meaning. When you feel you know *all* the meanings of *all* the words, go on to the exercise below.

EXERCISE 11A

From the four choices following each phrase or sentence, you are to circle the letter preceding the one that is closest in meaning to the italicized word. Where the same word appears more than once, you should note that it is being used in different senses.

1. an *affinity* for something (a) reason (b) dislike (c) attraction (d) use

2. a close *affinity* (a) relationship (b) secret (c) watch (d) atmosphere

3. a *bacchanalian* feast (a) sedate and dignified (b) wild and drunken (c) to honor a person's success (d) to mark the passing of someone

4. *blasphemous* talk (a) showing reverence for one's country (b) showing reverence for God (c) showing irreverence for one's country (d) showing irreverence for God

5. a *decennial* event (a) occurring every 2 years (b) occurring every 10 years (c) occurring every 12 years (d) occurring every 100 years

6. to *expatiate* (a) be forced to leave one's country (b) be forced to confess one's guilt (c) speak at great length (d) relinquish a claim

7. a *homogeneous* group (a) highly-skilled (b) the same throughout (c) mixed (d) small and isolated

8. willing to *intercede* (a) marry a person of another race (b) take the place of another (c) plead in behalf of another (d) explain something to another

9. to *intercede* in a quarrel (a) allocate blame (b) remain aloof (c) take sides (d) mediate

10. She is a *linguist*. (a) expert on fishing (b) expert on family trees (c) expert on birds (d) expert on languages

11. to commit a *malapropism* (a) act of irreverence toward God (b) misuse of public funds (c) humorous misuse of words (d) treasonable act against the state

12. to become *maudlin* (a) foolishly sentimental (b) careless in one's dress (c) overly concerned with minor details (d) coldly distant

13. a *nugatory* agreement (a) worthless (b) binding (c) written (d) unwritten

14. to join the *pantheon* (a) group of persons in exile (b) group of persons most esteemed (c) religious order vowed to silence (d) elite group of soldiers

15. to go to the *pantheon* (a) main building of a college (b) holy river in India (c) temple for all the gods (d) wise man whose opinions are respected

16. a *plethora* of something (a) excess (b) shortage (c) large basket (d) small amount

17. to *smelt* metals (a) beat into thin plates (b) toughen by heating and cooling (c) draw into fine wire (d) purify by melting

18. to eat *smelt* (a) smoked salmon (b) small, silvery fish (c) pickled cow's-stomach (d) wild, coarse-grained oats

19. a *surrogate* parent (a) strict (b) absent (c) lax (d) substitute

20. a New York *surrogate* (a) prison warden (b) absentee landlord (c) judge (d) manner of speech

21. to *upbraid* someone (a) scold (b) put fine clothes on (c) look up to (d) tie up the hair of

22. *vocal* in support of something (a) quietly active (b) working secretly (c) speaking openly and often (d) working against one's will

23. *vocal* mannerisms (a) of the whole body (b) of the face (c) of the hands (d) of the voice

Check your answers against the correct ones given below. The answers are not in order; this is to prevent your eye from catching sight of the correct answers before you have had a chance to do the exercise on your own.

9d. 1c. 15c. 19d. 22c. 2a. 10d. 6c. 8c. 21a. 5b. 13a. 11c. 3b. 17d. 12a. 4d. 14b. 7b. 18b. 20c. 23d. 16a.

Look up in your dictionary all the words for which you gave incorrect answers. Only when you have done this should you go on to the next exercise.

EXERCISE 11B

Each word in Word List 11 is used several times in the following sentences to illustrate different meanings or usage. One of the sentences for each word uses the italicized word incorrectly. You are to circle the letter preceding that sentence.

1. (a) She felt a close *affinity* with the animals of the wild. (b) This dye has a marked *affinity* for wool but leaves cotton unchanged. (c) Is the universe finite, or does it reach to *affinity*? (d) The close *affinity* of music to poetry has often been noted.

2. (a) The *bacchanalian* orgies of the royal court scandalized the country. (b) The emperor Nero was more interested in attending *bacchanals* than in governing his empire. (c) *Bacchanalian* revels were originally held by the Greeks to honor Bacchus, the god of wine. (d) Huge quantities of *bacchanalia* were consumed by the drunken revelers.

3. (a) The wind grew *blasphemous* and tossed the little ship like a cork upon the waves. (b) You *blaspheme* when you mock God in that way. (c) Using God's name loosely is *blasphemous* and sinful. (d) It was wrong of you to utter such *blasphemies* in the presence of the priest.

4. (a) The *decennial* games have been held every ten years since 1882. (b) The club will be ten years old next month, and plans for the *decennial* are under way. (c) The princess received a large bouquet of *decennials* from the mayor's daughter.

5. (a) I was obliged to close the door in the salesman's face while he was *expatiating* on the merits of his product. (b) Her knowledge of the country enabled her to *expatiate* fluently on its present situation. (c) He has been an *expatiate* from his country for many years.

6. (a) Children are divided into classes of equal ability because *homogeneous* grouping makes for more effective teaching. (b) Absolute *homogeneity* in classroom groupings is neither possible nor desirable. (c) I would like the *homogeneous* haircut she has. (d) Milk is *homogenized* by having the cream blended into the milk to create a uniform consistency.

7. (a) The prisoner's wife *interceded* with the king for his release. (b) The western powers would not *intercede* in the Middle East dispute. (c) Her *intercession* in behalf of the prisoners resulted in their being released. (d) The guards *interceded* the message the prisoner tried to smuggle out.

8. (a) She is an accomplished *linguist*, fluent in nine languages. (b) The message was translated into *linguist* before being transmitted. (c) This book on the history of the English language was written by one of our greatest *linguists*. (d) Before the science of *linguistics* was developed, very little was known about the structure of language.

9. (a) Dropping the tray of food on Lady Dimwoodie's lap was a dreadful *malapropism*. (b) Referring to an "allegory" when one means an "alligator" is a *malapropism*. (c) Her frequent *malapropisms* were a source of amusement to all her friends.

10. (a) She grew *maudlin* after having a few drinks and reminisced tearfully about her former husbands. (b) The scene where the father is reunited with his son was written in very *maudlin* fashion. (c) He muttered a few *maudlin* words of sympathy in an attempt to comfort her. (d) The scene where the cowboy hero rides off into the sunset was a real *maudlin*.

11. (a) She produced a *nugatory* that proved she was the real owner of the property. (b) The contract was rendered *nugatory* by their failure to fulfill its terms. (c) The book is so obviously biased as to be quite *nugatory*.

12. (a) The Romans built the *Pantheon* as a temple for the worship of all the gods. (b) The poet T.S. Eliot occupies an honored place in the *pantheon* of letters. (c) His name will be *pantheoned* as long as people honor noble deeds. (d) Stone tablets in the *pantheon* honor the names of the illustrious dead of the nation.

13. (a) The city offers a *plethora* of attractions to distract one from one's work. (b) She had a *plethora* of excuses for not completing her assignment on time. (c) *Plethora* can be successfully treated with heavy doses of penicillin.

14. (a) *Smelt* fishermen can be seen casting their nets into the lake. (b) Tin is *smelted* by separating the impurities out by melting and pouring off the pure metal. (c) The pure silver is *smelted* into ingots of uniform size and weight.

15. (a) When the cub's mother is replaced with a *surrogate*, the young animal cannot tell the difference. (b) New York and a few other states have *surrogates*, judges who hear cases concerning the disposition of wills, estates, and guardianships. (c) He was recently appointed a *surrogate* bishop in the Episcopal church. (d) You cannot *surrogate* assignments unless you have prior permission.

16. (a) The sergeant *upbraided* the recruit for arriving late. (b) She *upbraided* her hair in a thick coil on the top of her head.

17. (a) The local residents were *vocal* in their support of the new measures. (b) Air is forced through the *vocal* cords, enabling us to speak. (c) He ignored the *vocals* of the crowd and continued with his speech. (d) She is an accomplished *vocalist* with a full, expressive voice.

EXERCISE 11C

From the four numbered choices, complete the following analogies by underlining the word that stands in the same relationship to the third word as the second word does to the first. An explanation of analogies is given in the Introduction.

1. linguist:language::jurist: (1) law (2) military (3) trial (4) war

2. biannual:½::decennial: (1) 1,000 (2) 100 (3) 10 (4) 1

3. solar:sun::lunar: (1) earth (2) moon (3) stars (4) planets

4. nasal:nose::vocal: (1) speech (2) words (3) voice (4) ear

5. carmine:red::verdant: (1) blue (2) yellow (3) green (4) white

6. quarto:octavo::4: (1) 1 (2) 16 (3) 8 (4) 2

7. irrational:reason::inanimate: (1) life (2) liberty (3) happiness (4) animate

8. decapitate:head::eviscerate: (1) hair (2) skin (3) entrails (4) limbs

WORDLY WISE 11

BLASPHEMOUS and sacrilegious (Word List 10) are words with broad and overlapping meanings. Generally, however, *blasphemous* refers to language that shows irreverence for God; *sacrilegious* refers to the violation, by word or deed, of anything that is held sacred.

Etymology

Study the roots given below together with the English words derived from them. Capitalized words are those given in the Word List. You should look up in a dictionary any words that are unfamiliar to you.

Roots: *pan* (all) Greek — Examples: *PAN*THEON, *pan*demic

theos (God) Greek — Examples: PAN*THEON*, a*theist*, *theo*logy

homos (same) Greek — Examples: *HOMO*-GENEOUS, *homo*nym

genos (kind) Greek — Examples: HOMO-*GENEOUS*, *genus*

Word List 12

ASPERITY	LACONIC	PSYCHOSIS
BANDANNA	MACHIAVELLIAN	STERLING
CONCLAVE	MARSUPIAL	SYNOPSIS
DEPOSE	MELEE	UTILIZE
FUSELAGE	NULLIFY	ZENITH
INFLUX	PAPAL	

Look up the words above in your dictionary. Note that many of them have more than one meaning. When you feel that you know *all* the meanings of *all* the words, go on to the exercises below.

EXERCISE 12A

From the four choices following each phrase or sentence, you are to circle the letter preceding the one that is closest in meaning to the italicized word. Where the same word appears more than once, you should note that it is being used in different senses.

1. to speak with *asperity* (a) complete authority (b) nervous hesitation (c) sharpness of temper (d) wry humor

2. a large *bandanna* (a) brightly-colored handkerchief (b) Latin-American musical group (c) tall, broad-brimmed hat (d) cattle ranch

3. to attend the *conclave* (a) private school (b) committee hearing (c) private meeting (d) religious ceremony

4. a *conclave* of cardinals (a) private retreat (b) meeting to elect a pope (c) committee that advises the pope (d) ceremonial ring

5. to *depose* the ruler (a) obey (b) succeed (c) support (d) remove

6. to make a *deposition* (a) sworn statement (b) determined assault (c) last minute change (d) slight error

7. a long *fuselage* (a) barrage of gunfire (b) curled and powdered wig (c) body of an airplane (d) cord used to detonate a bomb

8. the *influx* of visitors (a) hurried departure (b) total absence (c) thin trickle (d) mass arrival

9. a *laconic* comment (a) concise (b) unkind (c) humorous (d) polite

10. a *Machiavellian* ruler (a) weak and ineffective (b) bold and adventurous (c) firm and just (d) cunning and deceitful

11. *marsupial* creatures (a) able to live on land or in water (b) having pouches for carrying the young (c) egg-laying (d) having tails used like fifth limbs.

12. a sudden *melee* (a) whim (b) shock (c) brawl (d) decision

13. to *nullify* the agreement (a) draw up (b) make valueless (c) sign into law (d) enforce

14. *papal* rule (a) of a king (b) of a dictator (c) of a pope (d) of the people

15. to treat the *psychosis* (a) mild nervous break-down (b) severe mental illness (c) minor bodily ailment (d) serious bodily disease

16. paid in *sterling* (a) paper money (b) coin (c) American money (d) British money

17. made of *sterling* (a) pure gold (b) mixed lead and tin (c) pure silver (d) mixed copper and zinc

18. a man of *sterling* character (a) depraved (b) poor (c) dubious (d) excellent

19. a short *synopsis* (a) introduction (b) speech (c) summary (d) trial

20. to *utilize* the office (a) use (b) abolish (c) discover (d) understand

21. at the *zenith* (a) lowest point (b) beginning (c) end (d) highest point

22. to point to the *zenith* (a) position of true north (b) point in the sky directly above (c) position of magnetic north (d) point of greatest height above sea level

Check your answers against the correct ones given at the top of the next column. The answers are not in order; this is to prevent your eye from catching sight of the correct answers before you have had a chance to do the exercise on your own.

5d. 17c. 10d. 18d. 7c. 1c. 12c. 22b. 20a. 11b. 2a. 14c. 9a. 16d. 6a. 19c. 21d. 4b. 15b. 13b. 3c. 8d.

Look up in your dictionary all the words for which you gave incorrect answers. Only when you have done this should you go on to the next exercise.

EXERCISE 12B

Each word in Word List 12 is used several times in the sentences below to illustrate different meanings or usage. One of the sentences for each word uses the italicized word incorrectly. You are to circle the letter preceding that sentence.

1. (a) "I've no time for further questions," she said with *asperity*. (b) You have cast a grave *asperity* on my character by calling me a cheat. (c) He made no effort to keep the *asperity* out of his voice as he told us to leave.

2. (a) He took out a gaudily-spotted *bandanna* and mopped his brow. (b) She knotted the *bandanna* about her head and tucked her hair under it. (c) The *bandanna* consisted of two guitarists and a drummer.

3. (a) A great *conclave* of people had gathered in the square. (b) After one of the shortest *conclaves* on record, the cardinals chose a new pope. (c) A good deal of political bargaining goes on in the *conclaves* that precede the nominating convention.

4. (a) He was *deposed* as prime minister and sent into forced retirement. (b) As she could not appear in court, a *deposition* was obtained from her. (c) The witness *deposed* that the accused was with her at the time of the crime. (d) She *deposed* nearly two thousand dollars in her savings account last year.

5. (a) Airliners of the future will have no windows in the *fuselage*. (b) A *fuselage* of shots rang out when they raised their heads.

6. (a) New Orleans expects a large *influx* of visitors for Mardi Gras. (b) A sudden *influx*

of cold air indicated that the heating system had broken down. (c) People continued to *influx* into the city although all accommodations were taken.

7. (a) The river meandered *laconically* across the great plain. (b) "He won't be needing these," said the cowboy *laconically*, taking the dead man's guns. (c) Her *laconic* comments were listened to with care by the students.

8. (a) Unable to cope with the *Machiavellian* politics of the capital, they returned to the provinces. (b) By a series of *Machiavellian* maneuvers she was soon in line for the position of prime minister. (c) She is a *Machiavellian* at heart, despite her air of probity. (d) He was able to *Machiavellian* himself into a position of great power in the land.

9. (a) Kangaroos, wombats, and bandicoots are *marsupials* and carry their young in stomach pouches. (b) The kangaroo resembles the *marsupial* but is a somewhat larger animal. (c) Kangaroos and other *marsupial* creatures abound in Australia.

10. (a) The two men emerged from the *melee* with black eyes and bloodied noses. (b) They were told not to *melee* innocent travelers who were passing through town. (c) In seconds the bar was the scene of a wild *melee* in which everyone took part.

11. (a) Lack of support from other countries is *nullifying* our efforts. (b) The judge *nullified* the agreement as the signatures had not been witnessed. (c) You will *nullify* the engine unless you maintain it properly. (d) All the gains made in the last five years will be *nullified* if war breaks out.

12. (a) She is a student of *papal* history. (b) A *papal* bull is an official letter or order from the pope. (c) For many years there were two *papal* claimants, one in Rome and one in Avignon. (d) *Papals*, cardinals, and bishops from all over the world have met in Rome this week.

13. (a) A *psychosis* can be any one of a number of far-reaching and prolonged mental disorders. (b) If a murderer is found to be *psychotic*, he is committed to an institution for the criminally insane. (c) She is suffering from *psychosis* of the liver and must not eat fats in any form. (d) A *psychotic* can be a very dangerous person, as his sense of reality is grossly distorted.

14. (a) We received a pair of *sterling* silver candlesticks on our anniversary. (b) She is a woman of *sterling* character and can be trusted implicitly. (c) We exchanged our dollars for *sterlings* when we arrived in England. (d) To prevent loss of *sterling*, the British government is restricting foreign travel.

15. (a) The publisher asked the author to submit a *synopsis* of her new novel. (b) The radio gives a weekly *synopsis* of the news every Sunday evening. (c) The doctor's *synopsis* shows the patient to be suffering from nervous exhaustion.

16. (a) We should *utilize* the materials available rather than ordering fresh supplies. (b) A door was removed from its hinges and *utilized* as a table. (c) A politician should not *utilize* his position for personal gain. (d) To make concrete, you *utilize* one part of cement to two parts of sand or gravel.

17. (a) By 1935 Willa Cather had reached the *zenith* of her literary career. (b) The orbiting satellite reached its *zenith* exactly on schedule. (c) The *zenith* of the mountain is perpetually covered in clouds. (d) From the *zenith* to the horizon is 90°.

EXERCISE 12C

This exercise combines synonyms and antonyms. You are to underline the word which is *either* most similar in meaning *or* most nearly opposite in meaning to the capitalized word. Underline only one word for each question after deciding that it is either an antonym or a synonym, and write A (for antonym) or S (for synonym) after the capitalized word. Allow 15 minutes only for this test. If you cannot answer a question, go on to the next without delay. If you have time left over at the end, go back and try to fill in unanswered questions.

26 or over correct: excellent
22 to 25 correct: good
21 or under correct: thorough review of A exercises indicated.

1. GREEN . . . .
surrogate papal sterling verdant scion

2. VALUABLE . . . .
verdant laconic nugatory maudlin bacchanalian

3. EXCELLENT . . . .
nugatory didactic ambulatory potentate sterling

4. PATH . . . .
meteoric itinerary trajectory larva plethora

5. SUBSTITUTE . . . .
surrogate pantheon smelt psychosis larva

6. EXODUS . . . .
synopsis influx zenith cortege axiom

7. BRAWL . . . .
durance accouter upbraid venire melee

8. TRUTH . . . .
sacrilege misdemeanor axiom referendum symposium

9. NADIR . . . .
octavo surrogate bandanna zenith venire

10. SUMMARY . . . .
decennial melee asperity merino synopsis

11. REVERENT . . . .
blasphemous nugatory sterling papal magniloquent

12. REMOVE . . . .
influx disdain intercede depose deduce

13. SHORTAGE . . . .
optimum exigency cortege excrescence plethora

14. CHEW . . . .
masticate upbraid dote temporize parole

15. DEPRIVED . . . .
marsupial maudlin gratuitous bereft refractory

16. VERBOSE . . . .
laconic papal Machiavellian linguist homogeneous

17. MEDIATE . . . .
accouter nullify intercede meteoric impeach

18. NECESSARY . . . .
felicitous gratuitous blasphemous sapient tertiary

19. SCOLD . . . .
upbraid suffuse masticate expatiate bandanna

20. MIXED . . . .
vocal homogeneous bereft hirsute sterling

21. WISE . . . .
sterling surrogate maudlin sapient equivocal

22. EQUIP . . . .
emote accouter utilize venire indite

23. REVULSION . . . .
asperity larva affinity temerity cornucopia

24. SENTIMENTAL . . . .
maudlin vocal paregoric laconic rheumy

25. VALIDATE . . . .
dissimulate exorcise nullify upbraid clandestine

26. LURE . . . .
zenith nirvana surrogate inveigle intercede

27. SHARPNESS . . . .
   opprobrium asperity affinity pantheon trajectory

28. BLAMEWORTHY . . . .
   magniloquent marsupial halcyon verdant unimpeachable

29. SCORN . . . .
   utilize suffuse disdain smelt plethora

30. SEDATE . . . .
   nugatory ethereal impecunious bacchanalian novitiate

WORDLY WISE 12

The men of Laconia, a country in ancient Greece whose capital was Sparta, were devoted to strict military discipline and were not given to idle chatter. Thus, LACONIC came to mean "given to speaking little," a meaning it has retained despite the fact that the Spartans long ago passed into oblivion.

Sterling was the name his English subjects gave to the new silver penny issued by William the Conqueror. Possibly the term described some feature of the coin's design — stars or birds (starlings). It took 240 pennies to make a pound by weight, and the phrase "a pound of sterlings" became shortened to "pound sterling," the basic unit of British money today.

Besides referring to British currency in general, STERLING denotes silver of the same purity as that originally used to make coins, and is a standard of quality. From this use of the word comes the figurative application to principles or qualities conforming to the highest standard (a person of sterling character; a sterling lad).

UTILIZE means "to make use of (something already at hand)" and to extract benefit or profit from it (to utilize exhaust gases to increase power; to utilize one's opportunities). *Use* means "to make use of" by 1) making a practice of certain behavior (a police officer must use caution in making an arrest), 2) availing oneself of or employing (a carpenter uses a saw), 3) partaking of (they use neither alcohol nor tobacco).

The ZENITH is the highest point in the heavens, that directly above the observer. The *nadir* is the point opposite the zenith, that directly beneath the observer. Both terms are used metaphorically to refer to the highest point and lowest point respectively of any activity or state (the zenith of her career; the nadir of her misfortunes).

Etymology

Study the roots and prefix given below together with the English words derived from them. Capitalized words are those given in the Word List. You should look up in a dictionary any words that are unfamiliar to you.

Prefix: *con-* (with) Latin — Examples: CONCLAVE, *con*nect, *con*jugal

Roots: *clavis* (key) Latin — Examples: CONCLAVE, *clavi*cle, *clavi*chord

asper (rough) Latin — Examples: ASPERSION, *asper*ity

psyche (mind) Greek — Examples: PSYCHOSIS, *psycho*logy

ACROSS

1. to find fault with; to scold
4. pompously boastful
12. a continuous coming in large numbers
13. characterized by political cunning and deceit
14. a private meeting
15. the same throughout
17. the highest point; the peak
19. an expert on languages
21. to plead in behalf of another
22. to cause to have no effect
23. able to walk (7)
25. to remove from a position of power
28. sharpness of temper
29. a page-size six inches by nine inches
32. to purify (metals) by melting
33. a nymph inhabiting streams and lakes (7)
34. an animal carrying its young in an abdominal pouch
38. a severe mental illness
40. occurring every ten years
42. speaking openly and often
43. having no worth; valueless
46. of the highest standard; excellent
47. having to do with the Pope
48. an attraction to or liking for
49. a substitute or deputy
50. to reduce to pulp by chewing
51. slender and graceful (3)
52. a temple for all the gods

DOWN

2. marked by drunken revelry
3. a statement requiring no proof because its truth is obvious
4. a confused fight
5. done without good reason
6. brief and to the point
7. to make practical use of
8. a state of perfect blessedness
9. showing lack of reverence for God
10. to speak or write on at length
11. left saddened by a loss; deprived
13. foolishly sentimental
16. the concluding part of a speech
18. to lure into doing something
20. that cannot be doubted or questioned
24. to equip; to outfit
26. to regard as beneath one's dignity
27. a comical misuse of words
30. the body of an airplane excluding the tail and wings
31. a large, brightly-colored handkerchief
35. disrespect for what is sacred
36. a short outline of a story; a summary
37. an excess or overabundance
39. to spread over
41. a procession of mourners at a funeral
42. covered with greenery; green in color
44. an insect in its earliest stage after hatching
45. to draw out; to elicit (4)

Chapter Five

Word List 13

ACOLYTE	DUCTILE	OBITUARY
ATAVISM	ENNOBLING	PROGNOSTICATE
BEDIZEN	FLOTSAM	RACONTEUR
CANTO	GUBERNATORIAL	SYBARITE
CREVICE	LIONIZE	UNWONTED
DEIFY	MORATORIUM	

Look up the words above in your dictionary. Note that many of them have more than one meaning. When you feel that you know *all* the meanings of *all* the words, go on to the exercises below.

EXERCISE 13A

From the four choices following each phrase or sentence, you are to circle the letter preceding the one that is closest in meaning to the italicized word. Where the same word appears more than once, you should note that it is being used in different senses.

1. an admiring *acolyte* (a) glance (b) remark (c) letter (d) follower

2. the *acolyte*'s duties (a) altar boy (b) presidential aide (c) teaching assistant (d) night guard

3. an example of *atavism* (a) wasting away of the body through malnutrition (b) drawing a conclusion not based on the facts (c) reverting back to the traits of one's ancestors (d) total lack of concern for the feelings of others

4. to *bedizen* themselves (a) gaudily adorn (b) foolishly deceive (c) carefully protect (d) illegally enrich

5. the final *canto* (a) division of a poem (b) version of a story (c) appeal before the courts (d) scene of a play

6. a deep *crevice* (a) mountain lake (b) narrow crack (c) mystery (d) despair

7. to *deify* someone (a) take arms against (b) convert to one's own religion (c) treat as godlike (d) cut down to size

8. a *ductile* metal (a) capable of being drawn into wire (b) capable of returning to its original shape after bending (c) capable of being heated without loss of strength (d) capable of cutting softer metals

9. a *ductile* mob (a) dangerous (b) angry (c) easily led (d) loudly complaining

10. an *ennobling* influence (a) hidden (b) harmful (c) strong (d) uplifting

11. pieces of *flotsam* (a) unused ammunition (b) broken pottery (c) floating wreckage (d) heavy artillery

12. a *gubernatorial* candidate (a) for city mayor (b) for state governor (c) for the Congress (d) for the presidency

13. to *lionize* someone (a) torment cruelly (b) build up the strength of (c) avoid all contact with (d) treat as a celebrity

14. a requested *moratorium* (a) period of relative peace during a war (b) legally-granted delay in the payment of debts (c) prison sentence set aside on condition of good behavior (d) probationary period for a person taking holy orders

15. a six-month *moratorium* (a) period of frenzied activity (b) waiting period (c) suspension of activity (d) period in which a loan becomes due

16. a lengthy *obituary* (a) appeal to one in authority (b) list of official guests (c) speech praising an honored guest (d) notice of a person's death

17. to *prognosticate* something (a) diagnose (b) predict (c) fear (d) remember

18. a skilled *raconteur* (a) storyteller (b) gambler (c) athlete (d) hunter

19. He is a *sybarite*. (a) strict disciplinarian (b) servile flatterer (c) hardy, self-disciplined person (d) pleasure-loving person

20. *unwonted* haste (a) undignified (b) unaccustomed (c) unforeseen (d) undisguised

Check your answers against the correct ones given below. The answers are not in order; this is to prevent your eye from catching sight of the correct answers before you have had a chance to do the exercise on your own.

7c. 1d. 6b. 19d. 9c. 10d. 14b. 13d. 5a. 20b. 16d. 18a. 2a. 11c. 4a. 12b. 3c. 15c. 8a. 17b.

Look up in your dictionary all the words for which you gave incorrect answers. Only when you have done this should you go on to the next exercise.

EXERCISE 13B

Each word in Word List 13 is used several times in the sentences below to illustrate different meanings or usage. One of the sentences for each word uses the italicized word incorrectly. You are to circle the letter preceding that sentence.

1. (a) The *acolyte's* duties were to light the altar candles and prepare the communion wine. (b) She is still fairly *acolyte*, but she will improve with practice. (c) Admiring teen-age *acolytes* fought for the privilege of helping the champion.

2. (a) Our fascination with fire is an *atavism* traceable perhaps to our cave-dwelling ancestors. (b) He derived a certain *atavistic* satisfaction from holding and swinging the club. (c) She was known to be an *atavistic* and had been receiving treatment for her condition.

3. (a) The native chiefs were *bedizened* in feather cloaks and strings of gaudy beads. (b) We laughed when we saw the little girls *bedizening* themselves in their mothers' finery. (c) The wall poster showed the octopus, the squid, and other *bedizens* of the deep.

4. (a) "Stool pigeon" is thieves' *canto* for a police informer. (b) The poem is divided into twelve *cantos*.

5. (a) The seabirds nest in *crevices* in the cliff face. (b) A lightning bolt had *creviced* the huge rock cleanly down the middle. (c) We filled in the *crevices* in the walls before we began painting the room.

6. (a) The Incas of Peru *deified* the Spanish conquistadores. (b) Hitler was treated almost as a *deify* by the Nazi party. (c) The Romans regarded the *deification* of the emperor with polite skepticism. (d) We *deify* the stars of Hollywood, forgetting that they are human beings like ourselves.

7. (a) Copper is an extremely *ductile* metal. (b) He has no will of his own, and such *ductile* persons are often led astray. (c) The water is carried along this narrow *ductile* which empties into the storage tank.

8. (a) By showing an unselfish concern for others, we *ennoble* ourselves. (b) She was a great believer in the *ennobling* effect of patriotic love for one's country. (c) She discovered that being willing to die for her beliefs was an *ennobling* experience. (d) They had *ennobled* themselves of half a million dollars at the expense of those who trusted them.

9. (a) The ship was equipped with a new *flotsam* when it put into port. (b) Beachcombers make a living picking up *flotsam* washed up on the beach. (c) A close watch was kept for *flotsam* from the wrecked ship.

10. (a) From the four *gubernatorial* candidates, the people of the state will choose their

governor. (b) She was a state *gubernatorial* for eight years before entering the Senate.

11. (a) Hollywood stars are used to being *lionized* by their adoring fans. (b) The fickle masses are as quick to forget an author as they were to *lionize* him. (c) Animals kept in captivity find it difficult to *lionize* themselves when released.

12. (a) "Rest in Peace" was the *moratorium* carved on her tombstone. (b) Because of poor harvests, the legislature granted a three-month *moratorium* on all farm mortgage payments. (c) The newspapers have agreed to observe a *moratorium* on all speculation concerning the coming election.

13. (a) Most newspapers carry *obituary* columns in which the deaths of prominent citizens are recorded. (b) I knew nothing of her death until I read her *obituary* in the morning paper. (c) The newspaper will print an *obituary* of every gift received for its Christmas Fund.

14. (a) The doctor's *prognosis* is for a complete recovery by the patient. (b) The doctor *prognosticated* one teaspoonful of the medicine before meals. (c) It is a bold person who will *prognosticate* future developments in this field. (d) She was considered a pessimist by her contemporaries, but many of her direst *prognostications* have come true.

15. (a) He tried to *raconteur* everything that had happened to him since leaving the house. (b) She is a delightful *raconteur* with a fund of amusing stories.

16. To a *sybarite* such as he was, army life was bound to be distasteful. (b) He is self-indulgent to the point of *sybaritism*. (c) Her banquets were *sybaritic* affairs replete with such delicacies as larks' tongues. (d) The sultan's robe was of costly *sybarite* imported from Japan.

17. (a) The meeting broke up with *unwonted* haste as soon as the vote had been taken. (b) She is a most *unwonted* child with an I.Q. of over 140. (c) An *unwonted* softness replaced the hard lines of his face as he permitted himself a smile.

EXERCISE 13C

Niccolo Machiavelli (1469-1527) was an Italian statesman and philosopher whose book **The Prince** became a primer for rulers and politicians generally. It extolled opportunism, deviousness, and downright trickery as legitimate and necessary for the maintenance of strong government. As a result, the term MACHIAVELLIAN came to be applied to such methods and to those who espoused them.

In a manner similar to that used above to explain the word "Machiavellian," describe the origin of, and the story behind, the following words:

MEANDER (Word List 5) . . . .

. . . .

. . . .

BACCHANALIAN (Word List 11) . . . .

. . . .

. . . .

NEMESIS (Word List 5) . . . .

. . . .

. . . .

MALAPROPISM (Word List 11) . . . .

. . . .

. . . .

WORDLY WISE 13

FLOTSAM is the name given to wreckage of a ship floating on the surface of the sea. It is often found in the phrase "flotsam and jetsam." *Jetsam* is anything deliberately thrown overboard to lighten a ship in distress or to prevent it from going down with a sinking ship. The distinction was once important: flotsam went to the crown; jetsam went to the lord of the manor where it washed ashore.

The plural of MORATORIUM is *moratoria* or *moratoriums*.

Etymology

Study the roots given below together with the English words derived from them. Capitalized words are those given in the Word List. You should look up in a dictionary any words that are unfamiliar to you.

Roots: *deus* (god) Latin — Examples: *DEIFY*, *deity*, *deism*

canto (sing) Latin — Examples: *CANTO*, in*canto*tion, *canto*r

duc, *duct* (to lead) — Examples: *DUCTILE*, aque*duct*, via*duct*, con*duct*

WORD LIST 14

AGUE	EGOISM	NARCOTIC
BANAL	EXIGUOUS	ONOMATOPOEIA
BOON	GLOAMING	PROPOUND
CLAIRVOYANT	IMPROPRIETY	RAPPROCHEMENT
CYST	LUPINE	TALISMAN
DEMAGOGUE		

Look up the words above in your dictionary. Note that many of them have more than one meaning. When you feel that you know *all* the meanings of *all* the words, go on to the following exercises.

EXERCISE 14A

From the four choices following each phrase or sentence, you are to circle the letter preceding the one that is closest in meaning to the italicized word. Where the same word appears more than once, you should note that it is being used in different senses.

1. to cure the *ague* (a) fever (b) backache (c) stomachache (d) open sore

2. a *banal* remark (a) encouraging (b) threatening (c) cryptic (d) trite

3. It was a *boon*. (a) shocking display of rudeness (b) welcome benefit (c) serious inconvenience (d) mild reprimand

4. to grant a *boon* (a) right to buy and sell (b) allowance (c) request (d) degree

5. a *boon* companion (a) secretive (b) traveling (c) treacherous (d) close

6. to be *clairvoyant* (a) supposedly able to communicate with spirits (b) supposedly able to perceive things not ordinarily present to the senses (c) supposedly able to heal by touching (d) supposedly able to transmit and receive thoughts

7. to remove the *cyst* (a) diseased bodily organ (b) small, pouchlike growth (c) area of dead skin (d) protective covering

8. He is a *demagogue*. (a) teacher (b) believer in democracy (c) rabble-rouser (d) diplomat

9. to defend *egoism* (a) the belief that all people are basically equal (b) the belief that nothing exists outside oneself (c) the belief in the immortality of the soul (d) the belief in the all-importance of oneself.

10. an *exiguous* amount (a) unlimited (b) large (c) sufficient (d) scanty

11. in the *gloaming* (a) shallow water (b) tall grass (c) twilight (d) light of dawn

12. the guest's *impropriety* (a) small business (b) improper act (c) savings (d) witty remark

13. a *lupine* ferocity (a) unbridled (b) blood-chilling (c) tigerish (d) wolflike

14. a powerful *narcotic* (a) spring trap (b) military unit (c) physique (d) drug

15. a clever use of *onomatopoeia* (a) words used metaphorically (b) words beginning with the same sound (c) words having the same vowel sound (d) words imitative of natural sounds

16. to *propound* a solution (a) propose (b) reject (c) consider (d) debate

17. a *rapprochement* between them (a) state of mutual suspicion (b) establishment of friendly relations (c) secret and illegal agreement (d) comical misunderstanding

18. to carry a *talisman* (a) goodwill offering (b) unwanted burden (c) good-luck charm (d) sturdy walking stick.

Check you answers against the correct ones given below. The answers are not in order; this is to prevent your eye from catching sight of the correct answers before you have had a chance to do the exercise on your own.

10d. 14d. 13d. 5d. 16a. 18c. 2d. 11c. 4c. 12b. 3b. 15d. 8c. 17b. 7b. 1a. 6b. 9d.

Look up in your dictionary all the words for which you gave incorrect answers. Only when you have done this should you go on to the next exercise.

EXERCISE 14B

Each word in Word List 14 is used several times in the following sentences to illustrate different meanings or usage. One of the sentences for each word uses the italicized word incorrectly. You are to circle the letter preceding that sentence.

1. (a) An *ague* is marked by chills, fever, and sweating, and is often malarial in origin. (b) People who have contracted malaria may suffer *agues* for years afterwards. (c) She was feeling slightly *ague* and decided to retire early.

2. (a) The *banality* of some advertising jingles is beyond belief. (b) He smiled *banally* when I asked him what he wanted. (c) We had expected a rousing speech, but all we got were a few *banal* utterances.

3. (a) This mild weather is a real *boon* to the farmers. (b) The queen promised to grant the *boon* that the young knight requested. (c) They have been *boon* companions since childhood. (d) A sharp reduction in taxes is expected to cause the economy to *boon.*

4. (a) He demonstrated his *claivoyance* by "seeing" his wife injure herself although she was hundreds of miles away. (b) Her ability to *clairvoyant* amazes everyone who knows her. (c) "How do you expect me to know what they're doing?" she said. "I'm not *clairvoyant.*"

5. (a) The doctor removed the *cyst* that was growing in the corner of his eye. (b) The doctor made a small *cyst* in the patient's neck with a scalpel.

6. (a) She made a *demagogic* attack on all the institutions we hold dear. (b) The meeting was held in the largest *demagogue* in the city. (c) His appeals to the people's prejudices show him for the *demagogue* he is. (d) Hitler's rise to power was a tribute more to his *demagoguery* than to the good sense of the German people.

7. (a) Although she calls herself an *egoist,* she is always willing to help others. (b) This book offers an *egoistic* explanation for the rise of capitalism. (c) "Least said, soonest mended" is an *egoism* containing much truth. (d) He cultivates his *egoism* and steadfastly refuses to see the needs of others.

8. (a) The heavy furs they wore would keep them warm in the most *exiguous* weather. (b) The reindeer feed on the *exiguous* growths of moss and lichen. (c) The old couple's means are *exiguous* and do not allow many luxuries.

9. (a) The children were *gloaming* with delight at the treats in store for them. (b) She loved to walk in the *gloaming*, listening to the song of the birds. (c) He left before dawn to work in the fields and returned in the *gloaming*.

10. (a) She has no idea how to behave and commits many *improprieties*. (b) Writing "principal" when we mean "principle" is an *impropriety* of language. (c) The governor thought it no *impropriety* to accept gifts from those seeking favors. (d) He was in a state of complete *impropriety* when the police arrested him.

11. (a) The sudden, *lupine* howls from outside the cabin chilled our blood. (b) The female *lupine* hunted for food for her hungry cubs. (c) The corners of his mouth were raised in a *lupine* snarl.

12. (a) The *narcotic* effects of this drug are not yet fully understood. (b) The doctor gave the patient a mild *narcotic* to ease the pain. (c) People addicted to heroin and other *narcotics* are in need of medical treatment. (d) When they saw needle marks on her arm, the police knew she was a *narcotic*.

13. (a) "Buzz," "hiss," and "crack" are *onomatopoeic* words. (b) The *onomatopoeia* in the blackbird's song inspired him to write the poem. (c) Poets use *onomatopoeia* because of the vividness it gives their writing.

14. (a) The money was *propounded* by the police for use as evidence. (b) When Einstein *propounded* his Theory of Relativity, he was greeted with polite skepticism. (c) A number of suggestions have been *propounded*, and we will consider them all.

15. (a) Federal mediators hope to achieve a *rapprochement* between the warring factions. (b) Britons regarded the *rapprochement* between Spain and Holland with alarm. (c) She gave a mild *rapprochement* to his children for their selfish behavior.

16. (a) The carved stone was a *talisman* which, so they believed, ensured abundant crops. (b) His air of complete authority was a *talisman* whose magic never failed. (c) She was appointed *talisman* for the whole district.

EXERCISE 14C

In each of the sentences below a word is omitted. From the four words provided, select the one that best completes the sentence. Allow ten minutes for this test. If you cannot answer a question, go on to the next one without delay. If you have time left over at the end, go back and try to fill in unanswered questions.

18 or over correct:	excellent
14 to 17 correct:	good
13 or under correct:	thorough review of "A" exercises indicated

1. The town's .... sat outside the general store hooting at each other's tall tales.
   sybarites agues demagogues raconteurs

2. In New York all legal disputes concerning wills are heard before the .... court.
   surrogate moratorium sybarite decennial

3. Lacking a real God, the Romans tried to .... the emperor.
   plethora deify propound bedizen

4. She felt a deep .... with the creatures of the wild.
   ensemble affinity parole norm

5. .... metals are easily drawn out into wire.
   banal papal verdant ductile

6. It is some .... urge that makes us clench our fists when we are angry.
   clairvoyant onomatopoeic atavistic gubernatorial

7. Pieces of .... float up onto the beach at high tide.
   acolyte lupine gloaming flotsam

8. The speaker mounted the . . . .
and cleared his throat nervously.
probity expatiate axiom rostrum

9. Each . . . . of the poem has
sixteen lines.
conclave cortege canto accolade

10. She swore that her . . . . was
responsible for her good fortune.
talisman octavo bandanna pantheon

11. He is a confirmed . . . . who lives
only for his pleasures.
acolyte sybarite surrogate Machiavellian

12. I learned of her death when I saw her
. . . . in the newspaper.
prognosticate decennial obituary agenda

13. He shook as if stricken with a(n)
. . . . when he saw the ghostly
hand.
boon cyst ague atavism

14. The government has declared a
. . . . on arms shipments to the
Far East.
malapropism moratorium plethora fuselage

15. She had a . . . . of excuses to
justify her behavior.
halcyon plethora peroration melee

16. His . . . . speech aroused the
crowd to a frenzy of excitement.
gratuitous exiguous demagogic unwonted

17. Statesmen are working to achieve a
. . . . between the two nations.
talisman rapprochement plethora surrogate

18. There are four . . . . candidates,
each confident he will occupy the Governor's
chair in January.
gubernatorial acolyte marsupial ethereal

19. The natives . . . . themselves in
beaded and feathered costumes.
deify bedizen lionize depose

20. An . . . . softness suffused the
parents' faces as they looked at their baby.
ambulatory exiguous impecunious unwonted

WORDLY WISE 14

BANAL is pronounced *BAY-nəl* or *bə-NAL*.

BOON, meaning "request," is an archaic term; it is in everyday use in its meaning "a welcome benefit" (the fine weather was a boon) and in the phrase "a boon companion."

EGOISM is the philosophical belief that self-interest is the motive behind all conscious action. A person holding to such beliefs is called an *egoist*. *Egotism* (Word List 5) refers to a conceited preoccupation with oneself and is marked by excessive use of "I" in conversation. A person suffering from this condition is called an *egotist*. It will be apparent that *egotist* is a term of opprobrium while *egoist* is not.

Etymology

Study the roots and prefix given below together with the English words derived from them. Capitalized words are those given in the Word List. You should look up in a dictionary any words that are unfamiliar to you.

Prefix: *pro-* (forward) Latin — Examples: *PRO-POUND, pro*position, *pro*duce
Roots: *demos* (people) Greek — Examples: *DEMA*GOGUE, *demo*cracy, epi*dem*ic
agogos (leader) Greek — Examples: DEMA-GOGUE, ped*agogue*

Word List 15

ANOINT	EMISSARY	NOVENA
BANEFUL	EXTRADITE	POLYGAMIST
BRIER	GOSSAMER	QUIP
COGNATE	INCOMMUNICADO	STELLAR
DEEM	MENDACITY	TROUSSEAU
DIPSOMANIAC		

Look up the words above in your dictionary. Note that many of them have more than one meaning. When you feel that you know *all* the meanings of *all* the words, go on to the exercises below.

EXERCISE 15A

From the four choices following each phrase or sentence, you are to circle the letter preceding the one that is closest in meaning to the italicized word. Where the same word appears more than once, you should note that it is being used in different senses.

1. to *anoint* something (a) pour wine on (b) pour oil on (c) pour water on (d) sprinkle gold dust on

2. to *anoint* the king (a) make holy by putting oil on (b) make holy by sprinkling water on (c) make holy by sprinkling wine on (d) make holy by offering a gold crown

3. a *baneful* effect (a) beneficial (b) ruinous (c) gradual (d) delayed

4. a patch of *brier* (a) bare ground (b) thorny bush (c) desert cactus (d) clinging seaweed

5. a *brier* pipe (a) made from a curved gourd (b) made from fine, white clay (c) made from the end of a corncob (d) made from the root of a European shrub

6. *cognate* languages (a) foreign (b) related (c) modern (d) ancient

7. to *deem* (a) request (b) fear (c) believe (d) respect

8. She is a *dipsomaniac.* (a) moron (b) psychotic (c) alcoholic (d) thief

9. the king's *emissary* (a) attendant (b) agent (c) reign (d) co-ruler

10. to *extradite* a person (a) involve in some difficulty (b) prove the guilt of (c) get out of some difficulty (d) hand over to the power of another state

11. as delicate as *gossamer* (a) swansdown (b) a baby's first growth of hair (c) strands of seaweed (d) filmy cobweb strands

12. *gossamer* fabrics (a) warm (b) shining (c) sheer (d) colorful

13. held *incommunicado* (a) without being able to get in touch with others (b) against one's wishes (c) without formal charges being laid (d) as a witness in a trial

14. accused of *mendacity* (a) meanness (b) lying (c) cheating (d) cruelty

15. a Catholic *novena* (a) five-day period of prayer (b) seven-day period of prayer (c) nine-day period of prayer (d) eleven-day period of prayer

16. to be a *polygamist* (a) person who remains unmarried (b) person with two or more limbs missing (c) person of many talents (d) person with more than one wife or husband

17. to make a *quip* (a) witty remark (b) blind guess (c) halfhearted attempt (d) sudden lunge

18. *stellar* motion (a) of the atom (b) of the stars (c) of water (d) of heat

19. a *stellar* attraction (a) well-publicized (b) for which no charge is made (c) restricted to adults (d) of a celebrated performer

20. to assemble the *trousseau* (a) hunting equipment (b) bride's outfit (c) ship's crew (d) royal guard

Check your answers against the correct ones given below. The answers are not in order; this is to prevent your eye from catching sight of the correct answers before you have had a chance to do the exercise on your own.

7c. 10d. 16d. 12c. 3b. 18b. 15c. 1b. 6b. 13a. 2a. 14b. 8c. 11d. 5d. 19d. 9b. 20b. 4b. 17a.

Look up in your dictionary all the words for which you gave incorrect answers. Only when you have done this should you go on to the next exercise.

EXERCISE 15B

Each word in Word List 15 is used several times in the sentences below to illustrate different meanings or usage. One of the sentences for each word uses the italicized word incorrectly. You are to circle the letter preceding that sentence.

1. (a) The fishermen *anointed* their lines with whale oil. (b) At the *anointed* hour the high priest sacrificed two newborn lambs. (c) They *anointed* their bodies with suntan oil. (d) King David was *anointed* by the prophet Samuel.

2. (a) They failed to anticipate the *baneful* effect the new farming methods would have on the land. (b) The superstitious villagers felt her to be under the *baneful* influence of the devil. (c) The peasants were *baneful* of venturing out after dark.

3. (a) The *briers* grow so densely it is impossible to pass through them. (b) A pipe made of fine Algerian *brier* can cost upwards of fifty dollars. (c) A *brier* from the rose bush pricked her finger and made it bleed.

4. (a) She *cognated* for a moment before replying. (b) English and German are *cognate* languages. (c) The English word "tobacco" and the French word "tabac" are *cognates*.

5. (a) I would *deem* it a great favor if you would accompany me. (b) He *deemed* himself a good judge of character. (c) I will come if you *deem* it necessary. (d) She had come to *deem* a favor from the lord of the manor.

6. (a) She has a positive *dipsomania* for maple candy. (b) Doctors believe that *dipsomania* can be controlled if the patient submits to treatment. (c) He admitted he was a *dipsomaniac* and said he had tried many times to swear off liquor.

7. (a) She said she was an *emissary* of the Chinese emperor. (b) *Emissaries* of the two warring nations met in an attempt to negotiate a peace. (c) The president sent an *emissary* to answer the questions of the newsreporters. (d) When the king read the *emissary* he flew into a violent rage.

8. (a) This country has *extradition* treaties with most countries of the world. (b) Texas state officials *extradited* the robber at the request of Mexican authorities. (c) She managed to *extradite* herself from what could have been an embarrassing situation. (d) He was *extradited* from Florida and sent back to New York to stand trial.

9. (a) The bride's veil was as delicate as *gossamer*. (b) She wore a *gossamer* gown of finest lace. (c) Nothing was allowed to harm the *gossamer* dreams of their childhood. (d) They wore black *gossamers* which partially obscured their faces.

10. (a) The prisoner complained that he had been held *incommunicado* for ten days. (b) The prisoner was taken to a small *incommunicado* from which it was impossible to escape

11. (a) The metal's *mendacity* is increased by this heat treatment. (b) She had an air of *mendacity* that made me suspect her story. (c) Everyone knew he was lying, but he refused to admit his *mendacity*. (d) The *mendacious* tales of her exploits went unchallenged for some time.

12. (a) He whispered the *novena* over and over again in thanks for his safe arrival. (b) She is a devout Catholic and plans to participate in the *novena* that begins tomorrow.

13. (a) The Batak people of the Philippines are confirmed *polygamists* (b) The Mormons practiced *polygamy* until it was outlawed by the Supreme Court. (c) *Polygamous* marriages are still common in certain Arabic and African countries. (d) He was admitted to the hospital with *polygamous* injuries sustained in a fall.

14. (a) She should try to be more serious and resist the temptation to make *quips* at every opportunity. (b) He moved the *quip* of tobacco to his other cheek and spat accurately into the spittoon. (c) "I won't need this anymore," *quipped* the condemned man, handing his hat to the executioner.

15. (a) From analysis of *stellar* light, we can determine of what elements the stars are constituted. (b) Much of the play's success is due to its *stellar* cast. (c) Light from a *stellar* may take millions of years to reach our earth. (d) It will probably be hundreds of years before inter*stellar* voyages are undertaken.

16. (a) The bride-to-be decided to save her money instead of buying a *trousseau*. (b) The bride carried a *trousseau* of red roses.

EXERCISE 15C

This exercise combines synonyms and antonyms. You are to underline the word which is *either* most similar in meaning *or* most nearly opposite in meaning to the capitalized word. Underline only one word for each question after deciding that it is either an antonym or a synonym, and write A (for antonym) or S (for synonym) after the capitalized word. Allow 15 minutes only for this test. If you cannot answer a question, go on to the next without delay. If you have time left over at the end, go back and try to fill in unanswered questions.

26 or over correct: excellent
22 to 25 correct: good
21 or under correct: thorough review of A
                       exercises indicated

1. CUSTOMARY . . . .
lupine gubernatorial unwonted stellar sybarite

2. FOLLOWER . . . .
gossamer acolyte canto cyst demagogue

3. PRAISE . . . .
opprobrium canto deem extradite prognosticate

4. SUBSTITUTE . . . .
emissary boon acolyte surrogate extradite

5. VIGOROUS . . . .
gloaming sybarite effete gratuitous marsupial

6. ORIGINAL . . . .
synopsis banal brier stellar pantheon

7. TASTY . . . .
ductile nugatory magniloquent surrogate insipid

8. RABBLE-ROUSER . . . .
emissary demagogue ague incommunicado lapidary

9. BENEFICIAL . . . .
bereft obituary banal baneful trenchant

10. FEVER . . . .
ague dipsomania brier cyst quip

11. TIMIDITY . . . .
mendacity atavism onomatopoeia effrontery nirvana

12. PERMANENT . . . .
evanescent exiguous narcotic homogeneous maudlin

13. DISASTER . . . .
affinity cortege boon acolyte fuselage

14. PREDICT . . . .
propound prognosticate anoint bedizen deem

15. UNRELATED . . . .
banal cognate vocal sterling bereft

16. TWILIGHT . . . .
novena ductile moratorium gloaming zenith

17. LIKING . . . .
conclave boon antipathy asperity surrogate

18. TRUTHFULNESS . . . .
    mendacity egoism impropriety rapprochement infraction

19. WOLFLIKE . . . .
    gubernatorial dipsomaniac lupine baneful narcotic

20. HAPPY . . . .
    gratuitous disconsolate cognate laconic equivocal

21. VALUABLE . . . .
    mordant clairvoyant verdant cognate nugatory

22. ADORN . . . .
    lionize depose bedizen nullify smelt

23. ABUNDANT . . . .
    exiguous gloaming halcyon potentate sapient

24. CONSIDER . . . .
    venire exorcise inflect reinstate deem

25. DISHONESTY . . . .
    flotsam atavism deify probity rapprochement

26. DIRECT . . . .
    hirsute ennobling equivocal exiguous blasphemous

27. STORYTELLER . . . .
    demagogue clairvoyant gossamer novena raconteur

28. BEGIN . . . .
    prognosticate desist propound upbraid correlate

29. PROPOSE . . . .
    bedizen anoint deify depose propound

30. SATISFIED . . . .
    unwonted insatiable lupine sapient hirsute

WORDLY WISE 15

Two words with variant spellings are ANOINT (also spelled *annoint*) and BRIER (also spelled *briar*). The spelling given in the Word List is preferred.

The plural of TROUSSEAU (pronounced *TROO-so*) is *trousseaux* or *trousseaus* (each pronounced *TROO-soz*).

Etymology

Study the roots and prefix given below together with the English words derived from them. Capitalized words are those given in the Word List. You should look up in a dictionary any words that are unfamiliar to you.

Prefix: *in-* (not) Latin — Examples: *IN*COMMUNICADO, *in*sufficient, *in*satiable

Roots: *gamos* (marriage) Greek - Examples: POLY*GAMY*, mono*gamy*, bi*gamy*
    mono (one) Greek - Examples: *mono*gamy, *mono*tone, *mono*poly
    bi (two) Greek - Examples: *bi*gamy, *bi*cycle, *bi*focal
    poly (many) Greek - Examples: *poly*gon, *POLY*GAMY, *poly*phony

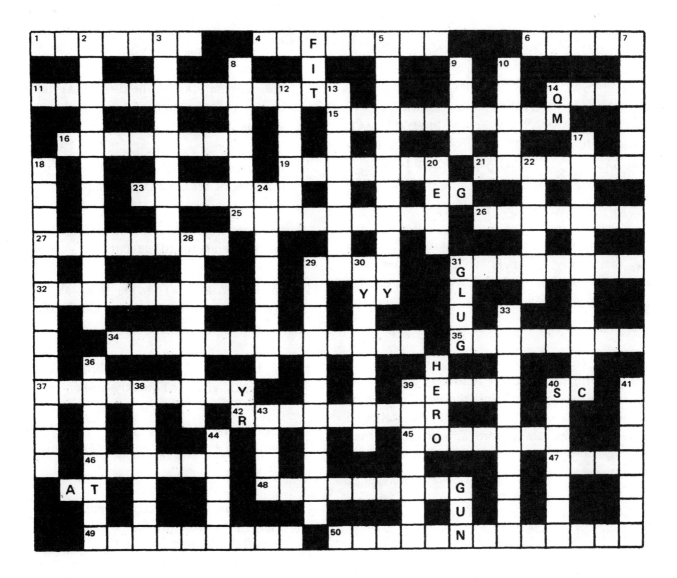

ACROSS

1. one who assists a priest; an altar boy
4. a fondness or attraction for (11)
6. dull and commonplace; trite
11. to predict; to tell the future
14. a clever or witty comment
15. a legally granted delay on the payment of debts
16. something believed to bring good luck
19. lacking taste or flavor (2)
21. a narrow crack or split
23. to dress or adorn gaudily
25. to hand over (a lawbreaker) to another state
26. wreckage floating on the sea
27. to set forth; to propose
29. a small pouchlike growth
31. light and filmy
32. a published notice of a person's death
34. without being able to communicate with others
35. twilight; dusk
37. untruthfulness; lying
39. to treat as godlike
42. a storyteller
45. coming from the same source; related
46. prayers held over a nine-day period
47. to wash (8)
48. uplifting; giving nobility to
49. a leader who appeals to the prejudices of the people
50. of or relating to a state governor

DOWN

2. use of words imitative of natural sounds
3. a bride's outfit of clothes and accessories
5. an improper act
7. of or like a wolf
8. to treat or regard as a celebrity
9. a welcome benefit; a blessing
10. a thorny bush
12. to put oil on
13. a representative or agent
17. one who uncontrollably craves alcohol
18. the establishment of friendly relations
20. to consider; to believe
22. a selfish belief in one's own importance
24. small in amount; scanty
28. a drug that soothes and induces sleep
29. supposedly able to perceive things not present ordinarily to the senses
30. a person devoted to luxury and pleasure
33. one who takes more than one spouse
36. unaccustomed
38. a reverting back to the traits of one's ancestors
39. easily led
40. of or relating to the stars
41. creating ruin; very harmful
43. a fever marked by chills
44. one of the divisions of a long poem

Chapter Six

Word List 16

ANTERIOR	EXPIATE	PANACEA
BLANDISHMENT	INVIOLATE	PREPONDERATE
CLIMACTERIC	LATTICE	REFUTATION
CONJUGAL	LEVIATHAN	SPOLIATION
DEPREDATION	OBJURGATE	VERBOSE
EMPYREAN		

Look up the words above in your dictionary. Note that many of them have more than one meaning. When you feel that you know *all* the meanings of *all* the words, go on to the exercises below.

EXERCISE 16A

From the four choices following each phrase or sentence, you are to circle the letter preceding the one that is closest in meaning to the italicized word. Where the same word appears more than once, you should note that it is being used in different senses.

1. the *anterior* part (a) front (b) rear (c) inside (d) outside

2. an *anterior* event (a) earlier (b) later (c) simultaneous (d) specific

3. to yield to *blandishments* (a) veiled threats (b) open threats (c) flattering remarks (d) constant attacks

4. the *climacteric* in his life (a) struggling beginnings (b) final days (c) fresh start (d) turning point

5. *conjugal* rights (a) legal (b) customary (c) inalienable (d) marital

6. to suffer *depredations* (a) humiliating experiences (b) acts of robbery and violence (c) long years of imprisonment (d) periods of doubt and uncertainty

7. the *depredations* of the disease (a) unknown causes (b) treatment (c) physical harm (d) various stages

8. to gaze at the *empyrean* (a) heavens (b) ocean (c) work of art (d) mighty conqueror

9. to *expiate* a crime (a) uncover (b) plan (c) make amends for (d) execute

10. to be *inviolate* (a) unable to speak (b) weak and defenseless (c) free from harm (d) given to fits of violent rage

11. an *inviolate* promise (a) unbroken (b) secret (c) lightly-given (d) quickly-broken

12. *lattice*work (a) crisscrossed strips (b) inlaid wood (c) intricately carved (d) embroidered silk

13. a *leviathan* of the deep (a) great mystery (b) scientific survey (c) find of sunken treasure (d) huge creature

14. to *objurgate* someone (a) rebuke (b) aid (c) ignore (d) sympathize with

15. a reputed *panacea* (a) source of great wealth (b) means of making gold (c) cure for all diseases (d) potion to keep one eternally young

16. to *preponderate* (a) be slow-moving and unwieldy (b) exceed in influence (c) add up (d) think over beforehand

17. an effective *refutation* (a) disavowal of interest (b) rule of human conduct (c) proof of error (d) welcoming speech

18. the *spoliation* of property (a) disposal (b) destruction (c) sharing (d) development

19. a *verbose* report (a) carefully delivered (b) incoherent (c) precise (d) wordy

Check your answers against the correct ones given below. The answers are not in order; this is to prevent your eye from catching sight of the correct answers before you have had a chance to do the exercise on your own.

8a. 4d. 14a. 17c. 15c. 13d. 2a. 11a. 6b. 19d. 7c. 5d. 3c. 1a. 12a. 10c. 18b. 16b. 9c.

Look up in your dictionary all the words for which you gave incorrect answers. Only when you have done this should you go on to the next exercise.

EXERCISE 16B
Each word in Word List 16 is used several times in the sentences below to illustrate different meanings or usage. One of the sentences for each word uses the italicized word incorrectly. You are to circle the letter preceding that sentence.

1. (a) The earthworm's head is located at the end of the *anterior* portion of its body. (b) The events described were *anterior* to the accident but are not necessarily the cause of it. (c) I suspect that he had an *anterior* motive for what he did.

2. (a) Highwayrobbers suddenly appeared, *blandishing* pistols and demanding all of our valuables. (b) She allowed herself to be *blandished* into giving her consent. (c) He succumbed to the *blandishments* of his children and agreed to take them camping. (d) She spoke *blandishing* words, hoping to coax him into changing his mind.

3. (a) World War II reached its *climacteric* in late 1942 with Allied victories at El Alamein, Stalingrad, and Guadalcanal. (b) Those were *climacteric* days for the nation as it underwent its most severe test. (c) Her election to Congress constitutes the first great *climacteric* of her early years. (d) In the final, *climacteric*

scene of the movie, the entire family is reunited.

4. (a) A restrained *conjugal* politeness kept the husband and wife from quarreling openly. (b) The husband and wife grew increasingly *conjugal* as they got older.

5. (a) The *depredations* of the Vikings along the eastern coast continued unabated. (b) Her pale face and wasted body spoke eloquently of the *depredations* the disease had made. (c) His mood of *depredation* was caused by the recent death of his only child.

6. (a) The poet speaks of the fiery chariot of the sun shining in *empyreal* splendor. (b) From the *empyrean* glory of heaven, Satan was cast into outermost darkness. (c) In medieval thought the outermost of the heavenly spheres was the *empyrean*. (d) Alexander the Great was *empyrean* of all the known world.

7. (a) They seek to *expiate* their sins by working among the poor without reward. (b) Payment of damages to the wronged party was considered a just *expiation*. (c) She received a sword-thrust through the heart and *expiated* without even a groan.

8. (a) She deliberately *inviolated* the rule forbidding new members to bring guests. (b) The confessions heard by a priest are *inviolate* and may be reported to no one. (c) Since the grove of trees was sacred to the Indians, the settlers agreed to keep it *inviolate*.

9. (a) The chalet's *lattice* windows gave it a quaint, old-world look. (b) A *lattice*work fence separated the two gardens. (c) *Lattice* was growing in profusion in the small garden.

10. (a) A ransom of five hundred gold *leviathans* was paid for the king's son. (b) The S.S. France, 1,035 feet in length, was the *leviathan* of the North Atlantic. (c) The *Leviathan* mentioned in the Bible is probably the great blue whale.

11. (a) It is useless to *objurgate* them when they don't know any better. (b) She relaxed her *objurgatory* tone a little before dismissing us. (c) He *objurgates* the modern tendency to disregard the traditions of our country. (d) Her spine was severely *objurgated* in the accident.

12. (a) Taxation can reduce inflation, but it is no *panacea* for our economic ills. (b) Only a complete *panacea* would remain optimistic in such a hopeless situation. (c) Panace was a mythical herb once believed to be a *panacea* for all diseases.

13. (a) State ownership will eventually *preponderate* in railroads and heavy industry. (b) The Democratic Party *preponderates* in the cities, the Republican Party in rural areas. (c) He *preponderated* the matter carefully before making his decision. (d) The Bolsheviks were the *preponderating* element in Russian pre-Revolutionary politics.

14. (a) Working harder is the best *refutation* of claims that you are lazy. (b) If you cannot *refute* your opponent's statements, everyone will accept them. (c) His clear *refutation* of your claim has convinced us that you are in error. (d) She is suing the newspapers for *refutation* of character because they accused her of taking bribes.

15. (a) Warm soapy water will remove the *spoliation* from his suit. (b) The *spoliation* of natural parkland by real-estate developers is condemned in this report. (c) Vandals continued their *spoliation* of villages along the frontiers of the Roman Empire.

16. (a) Include as much information as possible without being *verbose*. (b) She was such a *verbose* speaker that our attention soon wandered. (c) Many words have noun, adjectival, and *verbose* forms.

EXERCISE 16C

By adding or replacing prefixes as needed, construct words that are opposite in meaning to those given below. Underline the prefix of each word constructed.

1. APPRECIATE . . . .

2. UNDERSTAND . . . .

3. ASSENT . . . .

4. ACTIVE . . . .

5. TYPICAL . . . .

6. SYMPATHY . . . .

7. PROGRESS (verb) . . . .

8. INTROVERT . . . .

9. PREWAR . . . .

10. DRESS . . . .

WORDLY WISE 16

The antonym of ANTERIOR is *posterior* (a posterior event; the posterior portion of an animal).

Climactic relates to climax (the climactic moment of a play) and should not be confused with CLIMACTERIC, a critical period or turning point in life.

Note that EMPYREAN is both noun and adjective; *empyreal* is an alternative adjective form.

Livyāthān was the name for a real or imaginary aquatic animal of enormous size which was frequently mentioned in Hebrew poetry, including the Bible. From the connotation of strength and power of this beast, LEVIATHAN came to be applied figuratively to a ship of great size, or to a man of vast and formidable power and wealth (he was the leviathan of the country).

Etymology

Study the roots and prefixes given on the next page together with the English words derived from them. Capitalized words are those given in the Word List. You should look up in a dictionary any words that are unfamiliar to you.

Prefixes: *ante-* (before) Latin — Examples: *ANTE*RIOR, *ante*cedent

post- (after) Latin — Examples: *post*erior, *post*pone

Roots: *verbum* (word) Latin — Examples: *VERB*OSE, *verb*, *verb*atim

pondus (weight) Latin — Examples: PRE*POND*ERATE, *pond*erous, *pond*er

---

Word List 17

ASSEVERATE	INITIAL	PASSÉ
CARAPACE	JURISDICTION	RECIPROCATE
CLIQUE	LAYETTE	REPINE
CONNUBIAL	NEGOTIATE	TITIAN
DOCTRINE	OBVIATE	VIAL
EPIDEMIC		

Look up the words above in your dictionary. Note that many of them have more than one meaning. When you feel that you know *all* the meanings of *all* the words, go on to the exercises below.

EXERCISE 17A

From the four choices following each phrase or sentence, you are to circle the letter preceding the one that is closest in meaning to the italicized word. Where the same word appears more than once, you should note that it is being used in different senses.

1. to *asseverate* (a) remove oneself (b) swear falsely (c) break up (d) solemnly declare

2. a turtle's *carapace* (a) upper shell (b) lower shell (c) retractable head (d) skin

3. to resent the *clique* (a) rude remark (b) misstatement of the facts (c) small social error (d) small, exclusive group

4. *connubial* happiness (a) eternal (b) conjugal (c) heavenly (d) fleeting

5. religious *doctrine* (a) heresy (b) fervor (c) teachings (d) conversion

6. a sudden *epidemic* (a) cry of alarm (b) fit of coughing (c) stoppage of the heart (d) widespread disease

7. Truancy was *epidemic* in that school. (a) severely punished (b) discouraged (c) excessively prevalent (d) made easy

8. an *initial* test (a) thorough (b) first (c) final (d) superficial

9. to have *jurisdiction* (a) legal authority (b) immunity from arrest (c) a system of laws (d) the right to question one's accusers

10. a complete *layette* (a) set of clothes for a bride (b) set of clothes for a newborn baby (c) uniform for a newly-commissioned officer (d) set of plans for a building

11. to *negotiate* a treaty (a) give final approval to (b) stick to the terms of (c) settle the terms of (d) break the terms of

12. to *negotiate* an obstacle (a) be balked by (b) get around (c) disregard (d) set up

13. These bonds are *negotiable*. (a) worthless (b) nontransferable (c) tax-exempt (d) transferable

14. to *obviate* the need (a) determine (b) meet (c) question (d) make unnecessary

15. That is *passé*. (a) acceptable (b) first-class (c) out-of-date (d) up-to-date

16. to *reciprocate* (a) return in kind or degree (b) turn in circles (c) recover what has been lost (d) return to the starting point

17. a *reciprocating* part (a) moving in a circle (b) moving back and forth (c) fixed (d) revolving on its axis

18. to *repine* (a) grow sick (b) express remorse (c) feel discontent (d) take away from

65

19. *titian* hair (a) thick and luxurious (b) bluish-black (c) reddish-yellow (d) silver

20. to fill the *vial* (a) chink in a wall (b) leather wine bottle (c) empty space (d) small, glass medicine bottle

Check your answers against the correct ones given below. The answers are not in order; this is to prevent your eye from catching sight of the correct answers before you have had a chance to do the exercise on your own.

7c. 10b. 5c. 11c. 17b. 14d. 2a. 12b. 9a. 16a. 1d. 19c. 13d. 3d. 8b. 15c. 6d. 4b. 18c. 20d.

Look up in your dictionary all the words for which you gave incorrect answers. Only when you have done this should you go on to the next exercise.

EXERCISE 17B

Each word in Word List 17 is used several times in the sentences below to illustrate different meanings or usage. One of the sentences for each word uses the italicized word incorrectly. You are to circle the letter preceding that sentence.

1. (a) "I did not do it," he *asseverated*. (b) She was told to *asseverate* all connections with her former associates. (c) Despite his repeated *asseverations* I still question the truth of what he says.

2. (a) The turtle protects itself by withdrawing its head and limbs under its *carapace*. (b) Tortoises, turtles, and armadillos have protective *carapaces* covering their backs. (c) The young lady opened up her *carapace* when the sun began to shine.

3. (a) She complained that a small *clique* was running student affairs. (b) The opera singer had a *clique* in the audience hired just to applaud him. (c) These people are very *cliquish* and resent outsiders who try to move in.

4. (a) His wife was a most *connubial* young lady. (b) The old couple could look back on fifty years of *connubial* happiness.

5. (a) *Doctrinal* disputes have split the party into numerous factions. (b) "Let the buyer beware," she *doctrined* sagely. (c) He firmly believed in the *doctrine* "Might is right." (d) Her views differ considerably from orthodox Christian *doctrine*.

6. (a) The president referred to the ugly *epidemic* of rioting which has affected many of our cities in recent months. (b) The flu *epidemic* lasted over a month and affected nearly half a million people. (c) The doctor gave him an injection with an *epidemic* needle. (d) Sleeping sickness and malaria were *epidemic* in the region.

7. (a) *Initial* surveys show that oil is to be found in the region. (b) Please *initial* this notice to show that you have read it. (c) The new regime plans to *initial* many much-needed reforms. (d) We intended *initially* to include everyone in the project, but this proved impossible.

8. (a) The judge issued a *jurisdiction* ordering the immediate release of the prisoner. (b) The disputed area was placed under the *jurisdiction* of the United Nations. (c) The federal government does not have *jurisdiction* in this matter. (d) Since the accused is under sixteen, the case falls under the *jurisdiction* of the Juvenile Court.

9. (a) The baby wore a white *layette* trimmed with pink. (b) The mother-to-be had the *layette* ready weeks before the baby was born.

10. (a) He *negotiated* the deal on terms very advantageous to us. (b) Two of the canoes successfully *negotiated* the rapids, but a third struck a rock and sank. (c) *Negotiations* between the union and company representatives were resumed yesterday. (d) She will not sign the contract until she has conferred with her *negotiates*.

11. (a) His offer to deliver the package *obviates* the necessity of our going. (b) The United Appeal *obviates* the need for a large number of individual appeals. (c) Do not *obviate* from the instructions in any way.

12. (a) She used to be widely read, but most of her ideas are now *passé.* (b) He is an excellent swimmer but is barely *passé* in field sports. (c) The Riviera is becoming *passé* as a tourist area as more and more tourists are discovering Spain.

13. (a) *Reciprocating* engines are so called because of the to-and-fro movement of the pistons. (b) He was infatuated with her, but his love was not *reciprocated.* (c) The explorers accepted the furs and *reciprocated* by offering brightly-colored beads. (d) "You, sir, are a complete fool," the old woman *reciprocated* angrily.

14. (a) We must bear without *repining* the loss of all our hopes. (b) They *repined* to the lodge with the deer they had killed. (c) Her old age may be monotonous, but it is useless to *repine* over it.

15. (a) Jack Dempsey was one of the *titians* of American boxing. (b) She was a *titian*-haired beauty with a wide circle of admirers. (c) *Titian* is a reddish yellow named after the great Venetian painter who died in 1576.

16. (a) The *vial* contained the antidote to the poison. (b) The apothecary's shop was filled with *vials* containing exotic medicines. (c) The king's uncle devised a *vial* plot to seize the throne.

EXERCISE 17C

Complete the following analogies by underlining the numbered pair of words which are related to each other in the same way as the first pair of words are related.

1. anterior:posterior:: (1) front:rear (2) north:south (3) inside:outside (4) top:bottom (5) soon:late

2. dipsomaniac:alcohol:: (1) pyromaniac:fires (2) apothecary:drugs (3) addict:drugs (4) gourmet:food (5) student:knowledge

3. trousseau:bride:: (1) service:minister (2) groom:usher (3) church:cathedral (4) mother:child (5) layette:baby

4. carapace:plastron:: (1) turtle:tortoise (2) upper:lower (3) sea:land (4) inside:outside (5) mammal:insect

5. monogamy:polygamy:: (a) married:single (2) civilized:primitive (3) legal:illegal (4) one:many (5) bride:groom

6. brier:briar:: (1) smoke:pipe (2) tree:bush (3) bear:bare (4) anoint:annoint (5) e:a

7. highest:lowest:: (1) sterling:silver (2) conclave:enclave (3) biennial:biannual (4) zenith:nadir (5) flotsam:jetsam

8. canto:poem:: (1) painting:brush (2) writer:pen (3) song:singer (4) chapter:novel (5) writer:reader

WORDLY WISE 17

The CARAPACE of a turtle, tortoise, or similar animal, is the upper shell although the term is sometimes extended to refer to the entire shell, upper and lower. The *plastron* is the lower shell.

A CLIQUE (pronounced *KLEEK*) is a small, exclusive set of people which deliberately excludes outsiders. A *claque* (pronounced *KLAK*) is a group hired to attend a dramatic or musical performance and applaud loudly.

PASSÉ is always spelled with an accent over the "e" and is pronounced *pa-SAY*.

CONNUBIAL and *conjugal* (Word List 16) are used interchangeably although, strictly speaking, connubial refers to the married state (connubial bliss), while conjugal refers to the married persons (their conjugal affection for each other).

The Latin prefix *com-* may take one of several different forms depending on the beginning letter of the root with which it is combined. Before the letters *c, d, g, j, n, q, s,* or *t,* it takes the form *con-* because it is easier to say. CONNUBIAL, *con*comitant (Word List 18), and *consummate* (Word List 24) illustrate this shift of consonants. Similarly, before a root beginning with the letter *l*, *com-* becomes *col-*, for example in *col*lateral (Word List 2) and *col*loquial (Word List 8). The form *cor-* is used before the letter *r*, as in *cor*relate (Word List 9) or *cor*respond. In all its forms, the prefix means "together" or "with."

Etymology

Study the roots and prefix given below together with the English words derived from them. Capitalized words are those given in the Word List. You should look up in a dictionary any words unfamiliar to you.

Prefix: *epi-* (upon) Greek — Examples: *EPI-DEMIC, epigram, epidermis*

Roots: *jus;juris* (law) Latin — Examples: *JURIS-DICTION, jury, jurist*

dicere (declare) Latin — Examples: JURIS-*DICTION, indicate, predict*

demos (people) Greek — Examples: EPI-*DEMIC, demagogue*

Word List 18

BEATIFIC	INNUENDO	PHLEGMATIC
CLAUSTROPHOBIA	LACTEAL	RECONNAISSANCE
CONCOMITANT	LEAVEN	SEISMIC
COROLLARY	NOCTURNE	TONSURE
DOLOROUS	OPTION	VIVIPAROUS
ERSATZ		

Look up the words above in your dictionary. Note that many of them have more than one meaning. When you feel that you know *all* the meanings of *all* the words, go on to the following exercises.

EXERCISE 18A

From the four choices following each phrase or sentence, you are to circle the letter preceding the one that is closest in meaning to the italicized word. Where the same word appears more than once, you should note that it is being used in different senses.

1. a *beatific* smile (a) mischievous (b) blissful (c) forced (d) cruel

2. suffering from *claustrophobia* (a) fear of enclosed spaces (b) fear of heights (c) fear of the dark (d) fear of strangers

3. *concomitant* effects (a) trivial (b) accompanying (c) serious (d) initial

4. as a *corollary* (a) example taken at random (b) assumption not based on fact (c) necessary first step (d) proposition logically following

5. *dolorous* cries (a) mournful (b) joyful (c) ominous (d) excited

6. *ersatz* products (a) rare (b) naturally-occurring (c) substitute (d) common

7. to resent the *innuendo* (a) blatantly offensive remark (b) veiled, disparaging remark (c) unpatriotic remark (d) deliberately provocative act

8. a *lacteal* fluid (a) milky (b) thick (c) watery (d) murky

9. to *leaven* the dough (a) press and squeeze (b) roll out (c) bake (d) cause to rise

10. to *leaven* a speech with humor (a) mar (b) react to (c) modify the tone of (d) lengthen

11. to play a *nocturne* (a) musical piece suggesting night (b) musical piece suggesting the ocean (c) musical piece suggesting the country (d) musical piece suggesting joy

12. to have an *option* (a) limited liability (b) legal right of way (c) notice to appear in court (d) right to buy or sell

13. to have no *option* (a) money (b) choice (c) excuse (d) justification

14. a *phlegmatic* person (a) unreliable (b) excitable (c) cheerful (d) undemonstrative

15. to conduct a *reconnaissance* (a) test comparing two things (b) party guaranteed safe conduct (c) exploratory military survey (d) exploratory surgical probe

16. *seismic* disturbances (a) electrical storm (b) earthquake (c) civil (d) slight

17. a monk's *tonsure* (a) begging bowl (b) rough cloak (c) shaved head (d) vow of poverty

18. *viviparous* creatures (a) scaly (b) feathered (c) bearing live young (d) egg-laying

Check your answers against the correct ones given below. The answers are not in order; this is to prevent your eye from catching sight of the correct answers before you have had a chance to do the exercise on your own.

4d. 15c. 6c. 8a. 3b. 13b. 1b. 16b. 9d. 12d. 2a. 14d. 17c. 11a. 5a. 10c. 7b. 18c.

Look up in your dictionary all the words for which you gave incorrect answers. Only when you have done this should you go on to the next exercise.

EXERCISE 18B

Each word in Word List 18 is used several times in the sentences below to illustrate different meanings or usage. One of the sentences for each word uses the italicized word incorrectly. You are to circle the letter preceding that sentence.

1. (a) He lay on a grassy bank listening to the birds, a *beatific* smile on his face. (b) They waited until the sea became *beatific* before attempting the crossing. (c) A person who has seen God has been granted a *beatific* vision never to be forgotten.

2. (a) Sailors who suffer from *claustrophobia* should not volunteer for submarine service. (b) She is a *claustrophobe* and cannot bear to be shut up in a small room. (c) He shuddered as he entered the *claustrophobic* confines of the diving bell. (d) If her leg wound becomes *claustrophobic*, the surgeon may have to amputate.

3. (a) *Concomitant* with the belief in hell is the belief in heaven. (b) The country wished to remain neutral but became a *concomitant* almost against its will. (c) Paper rustling and fits of coughing are the inevitable *concomitants* of attending concerts.

4. (a) If the three angles of a triangle are equal, a *corollary* conclusion is that the three sides are equal also. (b) He offered his house as *corollary* for the loans he took out. (c) A massive highway construction program was a natural *corollary* to the vastly increasing number of cars.

5. (a) The liquid turns *dolorous* with age but can still be used. (b) Her songs were so *dolorous* that half the audience was in tears. (c) The forcible separation of children from their parents presented a most *dolorous* spectacle.

6. (a) Since the proper materials were not available, *ersatz* was used as a substitute. (b) *Ersatz* coffee can be made from roasted beech nuts. (c) The *ersatz* gaiety of the motel failed to stimulate the guests.

7. (a) His remarks may have been extremely *innuendo*, but there is nothing you can do about it. (b) Having no evidence against her, they resorted to *innuendo* to discredit her name. (c) The *innuendo* conveyed by his apparently innocent remarks was unmistakable.

8. (a) The baby animals are fed a *lacteal* preparation closely resembling milk. (b) Mammals have *lacteal* organs which produce milk for their newborn offspring. (c) The babies drink *lacteal* until they are old enough to eat solid food.

9. (a) Yeast is used to *leaven* the dough so that the bread will rise. (b) She *leavens* her air of gravity with an occasional witty remark. (c) The water in the reservoir had *leavened* to within a few feet of the top. (d) Baking powder is a *leaven* used in making biscuits.

10. (a) Moonlight shining on the lake inspired him to write this *nocturne*. (b) Bats and other *nocturne* creatures see poorly in daylight. (c) She began her recital with a quiet, romantic *nocturne*.

11. (a) We have an *option* on the house we looked at yesterday. (b) We have no *option* but to press on with our plans. (c) Given a choice between staying or leaving, we *optioned* to stay. (d) This course may be taken at the student's *option*.

12. (a) The wound should be thoroughly cleaned before it turns *phlegmatic*. (b) "Now, don't get excited," he said, puffing *phlegmatically* on his pipe. (c) Her *phlegmatic* manner had a calming effect on us whenever the situation seemed to be getting out of hand.

13. (a) An officer and six men volunteered to *reconnaissance* the enemy lines. (b) A *reconnaissance* team is employed to determine the position and strength of the enemy. (c) A light *reconnaissance* aircraft was shot down over the enemy lines yesterday.

14. (a) *Seismic* tremors from earthquakes can be felt thousands of miles away. (b) A slight *seismic* shook the area but no serious damage was reported. (c) *Seismographs* record the force and location of earthquakes.

15. (a) The monk's *tonsure* shone palely as he bowed his head in prayer. (b) His *tonsured* head and clerical robes showed him to be a monk. (c) The monks met each evening in the *tonsure* of the monastery.

16. (a) She smiled *viviparously* as I outlined the scheme to her. (b) Most fish lay eggs although a few species are *viviparous*. (c) Unlike most mammals, which are *viviparous*, the platypus is an egg-laying animal.

EXERCISE 18C

This exercise combines synonyms and antonyms. You are to underline the word which is *either* most similar *or* most nearly opposite in meaning to the capitalized word. Underline only one word for each question after deciding that it is either an antonym or a synonym, and write A (for antonym) or S (for synonym) after the capitalized word. Allow 15 minutes only for this test. If you cannot answer a question, go on to the next without delay. If you have time left over at the end, go back and try to fill in unanswered questions.

26 or over correct: excellent
22 to 25 correct: good
21 or under correct: thorough review of "A" exercises indicated

1. REJOICE . . . .
objurgate leaven repine refute expiate

2. GENUINE . . . .
dolorous concomitant seismic lacteal ersatz

3. HARMFUL . . . .
inviolate passé baneful connubial empyrean

4. FRONT . . . .
option corollary carapace anterior homogeneous

5. DEMONSTRATIVE . . .
phlegmatic blasphemous papal gratuitous sterling

6. TRITE . . . .
verbose banal clique initial seismic

7. COMMEND . . . .
objurgate obviate intercede influx suffuse

8. BOLDNESS . . . .
doctrine temerity depredation claustrophobia climacteric

9. MILKY . . . .
homogeneous titian lacteal empyrean nugatory

10. TERSE . . . .
concomitant verbose beatific bereft maudlin

11. PLENTIFUL....
homogeneous empyrean passé exiguous dolorous

12. NECESSITATE....
leaven reciprocate inveigle expatiate obviate

13. CUSTOMARY....
inviolate anterior initial nugatory unwonted

14. CONNUBIAL....
nugatory titian conjugal phlegmatic marsupial

15. CONFIRMATION....
blandishment refutation clique epidemic lattice

16. DESTRUCTION....
innuendo corollary carapace spoliation epidemic

17. HAPPY....
ersatz dolorous didactic ethereal panegyric

18. SPOLIATION....
incantation malapropism jurisdiction climacteric depredation

19. RELATED....
cognate anterior ethereal hirsute equivocal

20. BLISSFUL....
verbose beatific ersatz didactic colloquial

21. TALKATIVE....
empirical vernacular connubial laconic halcyon

22. SHORTAGE....
depredation doctrine innuendo option plethora

23. CURE-ALL....
lattice panacea claustrophobia fey firmament

24. GREEN....
nemesis lacteal tonsure verdant halcyon

25. WORSEN....
exacerbate reciprocate educe pontificate dissimulate

26. SWEAR....
obviate negotiate asseverate educe exculpate

27. FINAL....
beatific phlegmatic didactic initial probity

28. COMBINE....
negotiate expiate coalesce dissimulate inflect

29. SKY....
empyrean leviathan ethereal lunar panegyric

30. CHEW....
dissemble objurgate pulsate masticate eviscerate

WORDLY WISE 18

Optimum (Word List 4) is derived from the Latin *optimus*, meaning "best" and was brought into the English language during the 19th century to serve the needs of scientists. It describes the degree of light, heat, moisture, or other condition most favorable for growth, reproduction, or other vital processes of an organism, or the greatest degree of something obtained under specified conditions (the optimum temperature for incubation; the optimum safe speed given various road conditions). OPTION, based on the Latin *optare,* ("to choose") means a power or privilege of making a choice in some situation, and came into English from the French *option* during the 17th century.

Phlegm was one of the four bodily humors believed in medieval times to affect one's disposition. An excess of phlegm made one PHLEGMATIC (not easily excited; undemonstrative). Similarly, an excess of blood made one *sanguine* (cheerful); an excess of choler made one *choleric* (easily angered); and an excess of melancholer (black bile) made one *melancholy* (sad). When the four humors were in balance, one was said to be in good humor.

RECONNAISSANCE is both noun and adjective; the verb form is *reconnoiter* (The reconnaissance party will reconnoiter the enemy lines).

Etymology

Study the roots given below together with the English words derived from them. Capitalized words are those given in the Word List. You should look up in a dictionary any words unfamiliar to you.

Roots: *phobos* (fear) Greek — CLAUSTRO-*PHOBIA*, agora*phobia* (fear of open spaces)

claustron (closed) Latin — Examples: *CLAUSTRO*PHOBIA, en*close*

vivis (alive) Latin — Examples: *VI-VIP*AROUS, *vivid*, *viv*acious

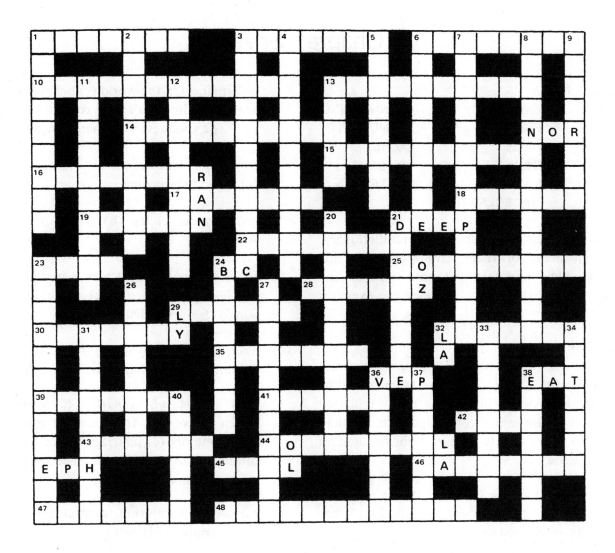

ACROSS

1. to make unnecessary
3. a husband whose wife is unfaithful (7)
6. a musical piece suggestive of night
10. legal authority over others
13. slow to be aroused; undemonstrative
14. bearing live young rather than eggs
15. deliberate destruction
16. situated at the front
17. a set of clothes for a newborn baby
18. the right to choose or to buy
19. a rich reddish-yellow color
22. indirect and disparaging comment
23. a welcome benefit; a blessing (14)
25. a proposition following from one already proved
28. used as a substitute; artificial
29. to cause (dough) to rise
30. to cause to have no effect (12)
32. of or relating to milk
35. of or at the beginning
39. of or caused by an earthquake
41. to feel or express discontent
42. a clever or witty comment (15)
43. an alarm bell or warning (1)
44. of or relating to marriage
45. a small glass medicine bottle
46. an upper shell, as of a turtle
47. a shaved part of the head, as of a monk
48. to surpass in weight, power or influence

DOWN

1. to rebuke; to find fault with
2. to declare solemnly
3. a turning point in one's life; a crucial period
4. going along with; accompanying
5. sorrowful; mournful
6. to discuss with a view to reaching agreement
7. a deep fear of enclosed spaces
8. an exploratory military survey
9. the heavens; the firmament (poetic)
11. proof of falsehood or error
12. free from harm
13. out of date; old-fashioned
20. an act of robbery or plunder
21. a set of teachings, beliefs, or principles
23. a coaxing or flattering remark
24. blessed; blissful
26. a prevalent and rapidly spreading disease
27. to return in kind or degree
31. any huge sea-animal or ship
33. of or relating to marriage; marital
34. an open framework of crossed stripping
36. using too many words; wordy
37. a supposed remedy for all ills
38. to make amends; to atone for
40. a small, exclusive circle of people

Chapter Seven

Word List 19

ACCRUE	FATALISM	OVERWEENING
BREVITY	FULGENT	PROMULGATE
CELERITY	GELID	SACHET
COMPOSURE	IMBECILE	STRIDENT
COTERIE	KAYAK	VORTEX
DISSECT	MISCEGENATION	

Look up the words above in your dictionary. Note that many of them have more than one meaning. When you feel that you know *all* the meanings of *all* the words, go on to the exercises below.

EXERCISE 19A

From the four choices following each phrase or sentence, you are to circle the letter preceding the one that is closest in meaning to the italicized word. Where the same word appears more than once, you should note that it is being used in different senses.

1. interest will *accrue* (a) taper off (b) remain at a fixed level (c) be added periodically (d) be greatly stimulated

2. the *brevity* of the speech (a) theme (b) purpose (c) shortness (d) conclusion

3. to do it with *celerity* (a) speed (b) precision (c) love (d) conviction

4. to recover one's *composure* (a) investment (b) self-control (c) expenses (d) health

5. to attract a *coterie* (a) challenger to one's authority (b) pretty young girl (c) large number of offers (d) intimate group of followers

6. to *dissect* the part (a) divide into equal parts (b) carefully cut apart (c) carefully put together (d) talk about at length

7. a profound *fatalism* (a) belief that things are steadily getting worse (b) concern at the unhappiness in the world (c) belief that events are not under man's own control (d) belief in the basic goodness of human beings

8. a *fulgent* landscape (a) dismal (b) stark (c) broad (d) dazzling

9. *gelid* water (a) icy (b) clear (c) murky (d) warm

10. He is an *imbecile*. (a) person in authority (b) highly-talented person (c) warmhearted person (d) feebleminded person

11. a skin-covered *kayak* (a) Japanese shield (b) Eskimo canoe (c) Indian tent (d) Zulu drum

12. laws against *miscegenation* (a) marriage between native and foreigner (b) marriage between minors (c) marriage between people of different races (d) marriage between persons previously married

13. *overweening* ambition (a) attainable (b) undue (c) determined (d) petty

14. to *promulgate* a decree (a) challenge (b) make void (c) proclaim (d) amend

15. a lavender-filled *sachet* (a) small bottle (b) small bag (c) small casket (d) small basket

16. a *strident* voice (a) firm (b) soft (c) shrill (d) frightened

17. caught in the *vortex* (a) storm (b) flood (c) avalanche (d) whirlpool

Check your answers against the correct ones given below. The answers are not in order; this is to prevent your eye from catching sight of the correct answers before you have had a chance to do the exercise on your own.

8d. 15b. 6b. 4b. 16c. 1c. 13b. 3a. 14c. 2c. 12c. 9a. 7c. 10d. 5d. 11b. 17d.

Look up in your dictionary all the words for which you gave incorrect answers. Only when you have done this should you go on to the next exercise.

EXERCISE 19B

Each word in Word List 19 is used several times in the sentences below to illustrate different meanings or usage. One of the sentences for each word uses the italicized word incorrectly. You are to circle the letter preceding that sentence.

1. (a) Some people believe that power *accrues* to those best able to make use of it. (b) The money collected was *accrued* to what we already had, making a total of ninety dollars. (c) Interest *accrues* to your savings at the rate of 5% per year.

2. (a) "*Brevity* is the soul of wit." (b) Because of the *brevity* of the storm, the young corn was little harmed. (c) The Catholic *brevity* contains the prayers to be spoken daily.

3. (a) We consumed the pie with a *celerity* that astounded us. (b) She could act with great *celerity* when the occasion demanded. (c) He was hailed as a *celerity* when he returned to his home town.

4. (a) He tried to *compose* himself before going in to greet his guests. (b) She quickly regained her *composure* and apologized for her angry outburst. (c) Joan of Arc's *composure* in the face of death won the admiration of the soldiers. (d) The final *composure* of the recital was a Chopin nocturne.

5. (a) The woodsman lives in a tiny *coterie* on the edge of the forest. (b) Every writer has a small *coterie* of devoted readers. (c) The governor is surrounded by a *coterie* whose job it is to protect him from outside criticism.

6. (a) We will now *dissect* the plant and ready it for the microscope. (b) The biology class is learning how to *dissect* a frog. (c) The Senate subcommittee *dissected* the president's budget proposals very carefully before giving their approval to

them. (d) Mother was an expert carver, and *dissection* of the Thanksgiving turkey was her responsibility.

7. (a) A *fatalist* is one who believes he is powerless to control the events in his life. (b) The loss of the harvest was a *fatalistic* blow to the hopes of the first settlers. (c) She took a somewhat *fatalistic* view of the misfortunes that beset her. (d) Their inability to improve living conditions induces a profound *fatalism* in these people.

8. (a) Her *fulgent* manner made me suspect that she was hiding something from me. (b) The sea was *fulgent* against a startlingly clear sky. (c) The gardens were *fulgent* with beds of riotously-colored flowers.

9. (a) The caribou makes its home in the *gelid* wastelands of the Arctic. (b) The air was *gelid* in the huge house, and there was no way of providing heat. (c) *Gelid* hardens as it cools and at very low temperatures becomes brittle. (d) He received a formally correct, though *gelid*, greeting from his political opponent.

10. (a) Psychologists have classified them as *imbeciles* with a mental age of four. (b) It would be *imbecilic* of me to agree to these outrageous demands. (c) The *imbecility* of these television programs is beyond belief. (d) She was *imbeciled* in a hospital for feeble-minded persons.

11. (a) Canvas-covered *kayaks* similar to those used by Eskimos are popular with hunters. (b) The Eskimos laced themselves into their *kayaks* and paddled away from the shore. (c) *Kayak* is used in the construction of canoes because of its great strength.

12. (a) *Miscegenation* is common in Hawaii where persons of different races mix freely. (b) Laws banning *miscegenation* have been declared unconstitutional by the Supreme Court. (c) There was a serious *miscegenation* in the accounts amounting to twelve thousand dollars.

13. (a) *Overweening* of children can lead to serious problems later in life. (b) Hitler's *overweening* ambition led him into reckless foreign adventures. (c) Her *overweening* pride would not allow her to confess her error.

14. (a) Orders were given for the immediate *promulgation* of the new regulations. (b) The Air Force Academy today *promulgated* the names of successful candidates. (c) He was severely *promulgated* for being lax in the execution of his duties.

15. (a) A lavender-filled *sachet* was always kept in the drawer to perfume the linen. (b) We watched the young children *sachet* across the room to receive their award.

16. (a) His voice became *strident* as he scolded us for being late. (b) She was always in a hurry, and her *strident* walk was a familiar sight to everyone. (c) The *strident* noises of the noontime traffic had given her a headache.

17. (a) Tornadoes do enormous damage to anything caught up in their *vortices*. (b) The small boat was caught in the *vortex* and was about to be sucked under. (c) The scandal reached ever greater proportions, with more and more prominent names being drawn into its *vortex*. (d) High wages are one of the chief *vortices* of prosperity.

EXERCISE 19C

A large number of countries have contributed to the vocabulary of the English language. Give the country of origin of each of the words below, all of which are now fully assimilated into English.

1. bungalow . . . .

2. tea . . . .

3. turquoise . . . .

4. cobra . . . .

5. brogans . . . .

6. camouflage . . . .

7. tulip . . . .

8. gong . . . .

9. tycoon . . . .

10. cigar . . . .

11. zero . . . .

12. stein . . . .

13. yacht . . . .

14. democracy . . . .

WORDLY WISE 19

DISSECT is a term in anatomy and means "to cut into for the purpose of study." *Bisect* is a term used in geometry and means "to divide (as a line or angle) into two equal parts."

The adjective form of FATALISM is *fatalistic* (a fatalistic view is one bound by the belief that events are not within a person's control). Do not confuse this word with *fatal*, which means "resulting in death or destruction" (a fatal accident).

A Germanic dialect known as Old English or Anglo-Saxon was introduced into Britain by invaders in the 5th and 6th centuries. During the next 1,500 years the English language changed considerably, but words of Anglo-Saxon origin still pervade our speech. OVERWEENING is a combination of the Anglo-Saxon prefix *over-* and the root *wēnan*, ("imagine" or "suppose") and means "arrogant, presumptuous, or exaggerated." Other Old English prefixes common in English today include *be-* ("make") as found in *bereft* (Word List 10), *becalm* or *bestir*; *fore-* ("before"), as in *foresee*; *mis-* ("wrong," "unfavorable"), as in *misdemeanor* (Word List 9) or *mistake*; and *out-* ("beyond," "more than"), as in *outmoded* (Word List 5), or *outlive*.

The plural of VORTEX is *vortices*.

Etymology

Study the roots and prefix given on the next page together with the English words derived from them. Capitalized words are those given in the Word List. You should look up in a dictionary any words unfamiliar to you.

Prefix: *dis-* (apart) Latin — Examples: *DIS*SECT, *dis*sent, *dis*jointed

Roots: *brevis* (short) Latin — Examples: *BREV*ITY, ab*brev*iate, *brief*

    secere (cut) Latin — Examples: bi*sect*, DIS*SECT*, *sect*ion

---

Word List 20

AMORPHOUS	FIORD	PLEASANTRY
BROMIDE	FUMIGATE	PROTUBERANT
CELIBATE	GENERATE	SEXTON
CONSANGUINITY	IMPORTUNE	TARIFF
CRUSTACEAN	MARINATE	WALLOW
EMBRASURE	OBTUSE	

Look up the words above in your dictionary. Note that many of them have more than one meaning. When you feel that you know *all* the meanings of *all* the words, go on to the exercises below.

EXERCISE 20A

From the four choices following each phrase or sentence, you are to circle the letter preceding the one that is closest in meaning to the italicized word. Where the same word appears more than once, you should note that is being used in different senses.

1. an *amorphous* mass (a) slowly-growing (b) shapeless (c) weightless (d) endless

2. an *amorphous* solid (a) acid-free (b) non-alkaline (c) salt-free (d) noncrystalline

3. to prepare the *bromide* (a) explosive (b) sedative (c) antidote (d) stimulant

4. a dull *bromide* (a) cutting edge (b) third-rate comedian (c) surface (d) commonplace expression

5. a *celibate* person (a) powerful (b) chaste (c) famous (d) helpless

6. to establish *consanguinity* (a) friendly relations (b) communication (c) kinship (d) willful intent

7. to identify the *crustacean* (a) scale-covered reptile (b) layer of rock (c) hard-shelled sea creature (d) animal remains preserved in rock

8. a high *embrasure* (a) lookout tower (b) recessed window opening (c) wall around a fort (d) official at a medieval court

9. a Norwegian *fiord* (a) gently sloping mountainside (b) small fishing village (c) small fishing boat (d) narrow inlet of the sea

10. to *fumigate* a room (a) let fresh air into (b) decorate with wood paneling (c) change the decor of (d) destroy pests in

11. to *generate* wealth (a) accumulate (b) share (c) spend foolishly (d) produce

12. to *importune* (a) spend freely (b) beg earnestly (c) work hard (d) waste time

13. to *marinate* meat (a) preserve by drying (b) tenderize by pounding (c) season by steeping (d) trim away excess fat from

14. an *obtuse* person (a) strong (b) stupid (c) fat (d) clever

15. an *obtuse* angle (a) between 0° and 90° (b) exactly 90° (c) between 90° and 180° (d) between 180° and 360°

16. to exchange *pleasantries* (a) small gifts (b) good-humored remarks (c) fond memories (d) food recipes

17. a *protuberant* part (a) bulging outward (b) riddled with holes (c) tubular (d) curving inward

18. the old *sexton* (a) matched set of bells (b) circular, six-paned window (c) device for measuring angles (d) caretaker of a church

19. a high *tariff* (a) lookout tower (b) tax on imported goods (c) tax on land (d) wall around an estate

20. I examined the inn's *tariff*. (a) bill of fare (b) record of guests registered (c) rating as to quality (d) scale of charges

21. to watch the animals *wallow* (a) roll about (b) communicate (c) grow sick (d) fight playfully

22. to *wallow* in luxury (a) desire to live (b) indulge oneself (c) decline to live (d) have memories of living

Check your answers against the correct ones given below. The answers are not in order; this is to prevent your eye from catching sight of the correct answers before you have had a chance to do the exercise on your own.

17a. 14b. 3b. 8b. 21a. 15c. 13c. 2d. 11d. 6c. 19b. 20d. 5b. 22b. 4d. 1b. 12b. 10d. 18d. 16b. 9d. 7c.

Look up in your dictionary all the words for which you gave incorrect answers. Only when you have done this should you go on to the next exercise.

EXERCISE 20B

Each word in Word List 20 is used several times in the sentences below to illustrate different meanings or usage. One of the sentences for each word uses the italicized word incorrectly. You are to circle the letter preceding that sentence.

1. (a) An *amorphous* cloud of dust hung over the site where the explosion had occurred. (b) *Amorphous* minerals are those without a crystalline structure. (c) What can be done about that *amorphous* conglomeration called the modern city? (d) He was deliberately *amorphous* in answering my questions.

2. (a) She asked us several *bromides*, but none of us knew the answers. (b) His nerves were jangled, and he was badly in need of a *bromide*. (c) "Every cloud has a silver lining," she said, as though uttering the *bromide* for the first time.

3. (a) He thought that the life of a *celibate* was a difficult one, especially for a man who would have liked to have children. (b) The bishop *celibated* the novitiates into the priesthood. (c) A Catholic priest takes a vow to remain *celibate*. (d) Not every person is suited to a life of *celibacy*.

4. (a) She regarded the loss of her fortune with an unconcerned *consanguinity*. (b) The person claiming the estate must be able to prove *consanguinity* with the deceased. (c) The relationship between parent and child is one of *consanguinity*; that between husband and wife is not.

5. (a) Lobsters are just one of many kinds of *crustaceans* found in these waters. (b) Barnacles, shrimps, water fleas, and crabs belong to the class *Crustacea*. (c) The prince's *crustacean* armor was proof against the spears of the enemy.

6. (a) She greeted her daughter with great *embrasure*, hugging and kissing her delightedly. (b) An *embrasure* is slanted outward to make the window look larger than it really is. (c) The *embrasure* was made wider on the outside to facilitate the firing of cannon.

7. (a) The coastlines of Norway and Alaska are indented with numerous *fiords*. (b) *Fiords* are generally deep, have steep sides, and are believed caused by the movement of glaciers. (c) It is impossible to *fiord* the inlet because the water is too deep.

8. (a) We had to *fumigate* the house to get rid of the cockroaches. (b) Hydrogen cyanide is a common *fumigant* used to destroy household pests. (c) The old gentleman was very impatient and *fumigated* at the delay.

9. (a) Wealth *generates* wealth. (b) By saving fifty cents a week, she was able to *generate* twenty-

six dollars in one year. (c) The candidate's speech failed to *generate* much interest in the town. (d) Niagara Falls *generates* enormous amounts of electricity.

10. (a) Business leaders find it hard to resist when the president *importunes* them to serve in Washington. (b) The mayor is weary of these *importunate* requests for favors. (c) The prisoner *importuned* the warden for a review of her case. (d) It was most *importunate* that I happened to meet him just at that moment.

11. (a) The meat should be *marinated* overnight in a mixture of oil, vinegar, and spices. (b) *Marinated* herring is a popular appetizer. (c) She was chief *marinate* on a British liner before taking up her present post. (d) Add a little more oil to the *marinade* before you soak the meat in it.

12. (a) A triangle cannot have more than one *obtuse* angle. (b) He is so *obtuse* that he thinks Columbus discovered America in the "Mayflower." (c) The blade is *obtuse* and needs sharpening.

13. (a) She greeted me with some *pleasantry* about the weather, but we didn't really converse. (b) It is natural for people living in the country to exchange *pleasantries* when they meet. (c) He gave her a small *pleasantry* as a memento of her visit.

14. (a) "Why don't we give a party tonight?" she asked *protuberantly*. (b) He was a short, fat man with *protuberant* eyes. (c) The thin faces and *protuberant* bellies of the children indicated that they were starving.

15. (a) The *sexton* looks after the church and performs such duties as the minister designates. (b) The ship's *sexton* cannot be used to determine position when the sky is overcast.

16. (a) *Tariffs* are imposed on imported goods to protect home industries. (b) The hotel is a comfortable one, and the *tariff* is not un-

reasonable. (c) We climbed to the top of the *tariff* and looked over. (d) A *tariff* of two cents a pound is charged on tea.

17. (a) The hippopotamus loves to *wallow* in the mud. (b) They are *wallowing* in luxury but refuse to give a dime to support their poor parents. (c) The bird gave a low *wallow* that could be heard clearly in the stillness of dusk. (d) Elephants find a shallow place in the river for use as a *wallow*.

EXERCISE 20C

In each of the sentences below a word is omitted. From the four words provided, select the one that best completes the sentence. Allow ten minutes for this test. If you cannot answer a question, go on to the next one without delay. If you have time left over at the end, go back and try to fill in unanswered questions.

18 or over correct:	excellent
14 to 17 correct:	good
13 or under correct:	thorough review of A exercises indicated

1. Clan members, claiming a common ancestor, are related by . . . . rapprochement   concomitant   miscegenation consanguinity

2. The lobster is a large . . . . much prized for its delicate meat. carapace sybarite crustacean leviathan

3. The best way to get rid of cockroaches is to . . . . the entire house. asseverate fumigate objurgate obviate

4. The . . . . of the peasants is due to their inability to control their own lives. egoism claustrophobia fatalism panacea

5. Her . . . . ambition will lead her into serious trouble. banal overweening strident amorphous

6. A small . . . . filled with lavender was kept in the linen drawer.
trousseau sachet embrasure lapidary

7. The government may impose a . . . . on any goods imported into the country.
tariff prognosis rapprochement corollary

8. It was the job of the . . . . to look after the church.
cortege talisman sexton tonsure

9. A . . . . is a narrow deep inlet of the sea with steep sides carved out by the action of glaciers.
vortex fiord kayak crevice

10. Interest will . . . . at the rate of five percent per annum.
accrue repine option nullify

11. Members of monastic orders are expected to lead . . . . lives.
viviparous connubial celibate overweening

12. The actress had a small . . . . who attended all her opening nights.
novena coterie surrogate conclave

13. The biology class is being taught how to . . . . an earthworm.
cognate dissect bereft conclave

14. It is useless to . . . . me with requests for help.
importune depose utilize doctrine

15. A . . . . quickly rights itself if it overturns in the water.
melee tonsure kayak acolyte

16. With interracial marriages increasing, ... no longer arouses the strong feelings it once did.
onomatopoeia clairvoyance miscegenation claustrophobia

17. You should . . . . the meat in a vinegar and oil mixture.
marinate ersatz leaven masticate

18. He said "Good morning" or some such . . . . whenever we met.
blandishment pleasantry malapropism surrogate

19. She is the . . . . of one of England's noble families.
vial scion axiom carapace

20. Icebergs abound in the . . . . waters of the arctic regions.
gelid verdant lupine climacteric

WORDLY WISE 20

FIORD is also spelled *fjord*. Both spellings are correct.

Sex, the Latin number six, appears in a number of English words, for example in *sextant*, *sextuple*, and *sextette*. SEXTON, however, is derived from the Anglo-French *segersteine*, meaning "sacristan," a church officer in charge of the sacristy and ceremonial equipment. A sexton today takes care of the whole church building and sometimes also has duties of ringing the bells and digging graves.

Etymology

Study the roots and prefixes given below together with the English words derived from them. Capitalized words are those given in the Word List. You should look up in a dictionary any words unfamiliar to you.

Prefixes: *a-* (without) Greek — Examples: *A*MORPHOUS, *a*theist
(review) *con-* (with) Latin — Examples: *CON*SANGUINITY, *con*spire, *con*sort

Roots: *morphe* (form) Greek — Examples: A*MORPH*OUS, meta*morph*osis
sanguis, *sanguin* (blood) Latin — Examples: CON*SANGUIN*ITY, *sanguine*, *sanguin*ary

Word List 21

BIENNIAL	FRUCTIFY	OSTENSIBLE
CAUCUS	FUSTIAN	PHYSIOGNOMY
COMPOSITE	GENTRY	PROGNOSIS
CONTIGUOUS	INGENUE	SHROUD
DIAPHANOUS	MIEN	UKASE
EPIDERMIS		

Look up the words above in your dictionary. Note that many of them have more than one meaning. When you feel that you know *all* the meanings of *all* the words, go on to the exercises below.

EXERCISE 21A

From the four choices following each phrase or sentence, you are to circle the letter preceding the one that is closest in meaning to the italicized word. Where the same word appears more than once, you should note that it is being used in different senses.

1. a *biennial* event (a) every six months (b) every year (c) every two years (d) every six years

2. to hold a *caucus* (a) hearing to investigate complaints (b) private political meeting (c) special runoff election (d) door-to-door survey

3. a *composite* picture (a) pleasing to the eye (b) formed of separate parts (c) of more than one color (d) portraying several persons

4. *contiguous* parts (a) scattered (b) complete (c) adjoining (d) separate

5. *diaphanous* garments (a) white (b) sheer (c) embroidered (d) heavy

6. a person's *epidermis* (a) susceptibility to disease (b) death notice (c) collected writings (d) outer layer of skin

7. to *fructify* (a) bear fruit (b) turn to sugar (c) become sour (d) dry up

8. a *fustian* manner (a) careless (b) precise (c) relaxed (d) pompous

9. the local *gentry* (a) person who does odd jobs (b) person responsible for keeping order (c) persons of high social standing (d) place where people meet socially

10. to play the *ingenue* (a) role of a clever trickster (b) role of a wicked old woman (c) role of a naive girl (d) role of a pretended invalid

11. a proud *mien* (a) soldier (b) boast (c) manner (d) parent

12. the *ostensible* reason (a) obvious (b) chief (c) actual (d) apparent

13. an ugly *physiognomy* (a) face (b) situation (c) threat (d) personality

14. a cheerful *prognosis* (a) manner (b) feeling (c) prediction (d) personality

15. a linen *shroud* (a) bandage used to support a broken limb (b) sheet for wrapping a dead body (c) cover placed over a coffin (d) robe worn by a priest

16. a ship's *shrouds* (a) sails used in a light breeze (b) ropes used to support the mast (c) sleeping berths below decks (d) flags used for signaling

17. to *shroud* the scene (a) picture (b) frame (c) reveal (d) conceal

18. the czar's *ukase* (a) heir (b) adviser (c) palace (d) decree

Check your answers against the correct ones given below. The answers are not in order; this is to prevent your eye from catching sight of the correct answers before you have had a chance to do the exercise on your own.

8d. 3b. 14c. 17d. 15b. 13a. 2b. 11c. 6d. 5b. 4c. 1c. 12d. 10c. 18d. 16b. 9c. 7a.

Look up in your dictionary all the words for which you gave incorrect answers. Only when you have done this should you go on to the next exercise.

EXERCISE 21B

Each word in Word List 21 is used several times in the sentences below to illustrate different meanings or usage. One of the sentences for each word uses the italicized word incorrectly. You are to circle the letter preceding that sentence.

1. (a) *Biennials* such as the parsnip have a life-span of two years. (b) This event is a *biennial* one because two years preparation is required for it. (c) She took a two-year *biennial* from her teaching post. (d) Gubernatorial elections have been held *biennially*, but the term of office is being doubled to four years.

2. (a) The doctor removed the *caucus* from his leg quickly and painlessly. (b) The state delegates to the convention are holding a *caucus* to decide whom to support. (c) The delegates *caucused* at seven o'clock this evening.

3. (a) From the different descriptions given by witnesses, the police formed a *composite* picture of the robber. (b) The knight in **The Canterbury Tales** is a *composite* portrait of men Chaucer knew personally. (c) She tried to *composite* herself with the knowledge that at least she had not lost any money.

4. (a) My offer to buy the house is *contiguous* upon the necessary repairs being made. (b) New Hampshire and Vermont are *contiguous*. (c) The lots *contiguous* to the shore are more expensive than those farther back.

5. (a) The veil was made of lace so *diaphanous* that it could be seen through. (b) These are but airy dreams, as *diaphanous* as wisps of morning mist. (c) They threw the stores overboard in an attempt to make the boat more *diaphanous*.

6. (a) The skin has several distinct layers, the *epidermis* being the outermost one. (b) The doctor took out an *epidermis* needle and gave me an injection. (c) The scratch was so slight it barely penetrated the *epidermis*. (d) Sun-bathers lay on the beach, their *epidermises* turning a bright lobster-red.

7. (a) Irrigation shall cause the deserts to *fructify*. (b) Our lemon tree will not *fructify* because the climate here is not warm enough. (c) The chef *fructified* the berries and served them with sugar and heavy cream.

8. (a) His face turned *fustian* when he saw how he had been tricked. (b) Despite her *fustian* appearance she is not at all pompous. (c) The much-vaunted eloquence of his speeches now seems unadulterated *fustian*.

9. (a) Only members of the *gentry* are admitted to the country club. (b) The *gentry* own the land, and the common people work on it. (c) We wished each other good morning and exchanged *gentries* about the weather.

10. (a) Her youth and freshness, together with her air of innocence, make her ideal for *ingenue* roles. (b) He is highly *ingenue* at getting what he wants. (c) The play calls for a romantic lead, an *ingenue*, and an elderly couple. (d) Appointing a political *ingenue* to such an important position was a great blunder.

11. (a) Her usual *mien* of solemnity had been set aside for the evening, and she was actually smiling. (b) He wore a *mien* of hardened steel to protect him in battle. (c) A monster of most horrible *mien* appeared suddenly before him.

12. (a) She's a very *ostensible* person and will be glad to oblige you in this matter. (b) The *ostensible* purpose of his trip was to visit his brother, but we knew he had a deeper motive. (c) She stopped by *ostensibly* to have a chat but actually to find out how much I knew.

13. (a) A person's *physiognomy* reveals a great deal about his or her character. (b) She is studying every *physiognomy* of the situation. (c) Her stern *physiognomy* was indicative of a disciplined mind.

14. (a) The *prognosis* is for the patient's complete restoration to health. (b) The *prognosis* is grave; patients rarely recover from this disease. (c) A sandy *prognosis* extended out nearly a mile from the shore. (d) He *prognosticated* that no good would come from the measures being taken.

15. (a) The body was wrapped in a *shroud* and buried. (b) Darkness *shrouded* the town. (c) She pulled off a number of *shroudy* deals that made her lots of money. (d) The *shrouds* run from the sides of the ship and support the mast.

16. (a) He can play the banjo, *ukase,* and guitar. (b) The *ukase* of the Russian czar had the force of law. (c) Totalitarian governments rule by *ukase* without regard to the wishes of the governed.

EXERCISE 21C

This exercise combines synonyms and antonyms. You are to underline the word which is *either* most similar in meaning *or* most nearly opposite in meaning to the capitalized word. Underline only one word for each question after deciding that it is either an antonym or a synonym, and write A (for antonym) or S (for synonym) after the capitalized word. Allow 15 minutes only for this test. If you cannot answer a question, go on to the next without delay. If you have time left over at the end, go back and try to fill in unanswered questions.

26 or over correct:　　excellent
22 to 25 correct:　　good
21 or under correct:　　thorough review of A exercises indicated

1. PROCLAIM . . . .
   inveigle educe temporize accouter promulgate

2. WHIRLPOOL . . . .
   influx vicissitude trajectory vortex venire

3. CONCISE . . . .
   disconsolate laconic acetic precipitous nugatory

4. SHORTNESS . . . .
   moratorium maxim brevity probity affinity

5. SUCCESSFUL . . . .
   unwonted trenchant ductile abortive circumspect

6. SHAPELESS . . . .
   amorphous blasphemous paregoric apoplectic fulgent

7. SEPARATE . . . .
   accrue macerate coalesce impeach depose

8. SHEER . . . .
   fustian felicitous tactile diaphanous magniloquent

9. SPEED . . . .
   asperity celerity phalanx antipathy embrasure

10. SUNKEN . . . .
    acolyte disjointed effete protuberant cyst

11. SEDATIVE . . . .
    axiom evanescent bromide mordant talisman

12. CONCEAL . . . .
    fructify expatiate indite inflect shroud

13. DAZZLING . . . .
    fulgent felicitous tertiary evanescent bacchanalian

14. POMPOUS . . . .
    specious fustian opulent exiguous protuberant

15. SHARP . . . .
    gratuitous lapidary disjointed ductile obtuse

16. SHRILL . . . .
laconic vibrant strident ethereal diaphanous

17. APPARENT . . . .
empyrean ostensible clandestine equivocal composite

18. SELF-CONTROL . . . .
panacea malfeasance itinerary composure flotsam

19. ADJOINING . . . .
contiguous collateral impecunious concomitant inviolate

20. FACE . . . .
bandanna frieze physiognomy scion gossamer

21. ICY . . . .
crustacean gelid rheumy panegyric lupine

22. DIRECT . . . .
equivocal decennial sapient refractory connubial

23. USE . . . .
intercede foment utilize dissemble anoint

24. PRODUCE . . . .
fumigate effeminate recant deem generate

25. SUMMARY . . . .
empathy conclave geneology mendacity synopsis

26. DEGRADING . . . .
ersatz ennobling didactic refractory viviparous

27. IDIOT . . . .
gargoyle scion imbecile palfrey emissary

28. EVEN . . . .
equable precipitous evanescent passe' beatific

29. FOOLISH . . . .
contiguous bereft svelte dolorous sapient

30. BEARING . . . .
effrontery mien motif temerity cortege

WORDLY WISE 21

A BIENNIAL event occurs every two years; a *biannual* event occurs twice a year. These two terms are easily confused with each other.

The word CAUCUS appears in John Adams's diary for the year 1763, and it may have originated in New England, having been borrowed from the Indians; perhaps it was based on the Algonkian word *cau-cau-as-u* meaning "one who gives counsel or incites to action." In the United States, a caucus typically is a meeting of a political party's leaders to select candidates or determine party policy.

PHYSIOGNOMY is a synonym for *face* only insofar as a face reveals character. "His physiognomy reveals great strength of character" is correct; "She was struck in the physiognomy by the ball" is incorrect.

A PROGNOSIS (plural *prognoses*) is (1) a prediction as to the course of a disease, (2) a prediction. To *prognosticate* is to make a prognosis; a *prognostication* is the same as a prognosis in its more general meaning of something predicted. A *diagnosis* is the determination of the nature of a disease.

Etymology

Study the roots and prefix given below together with the English words derived from them. Capitalized words are those given in the Word List. You should look up in a dictionary any words that are unfamiliar to you.

Prefix: (review) *epi-* (upon) Greek — Examples: *EPI*DERMIS, *epi*demic, *epi*taph

Roots: *dermis* (skin) Greek — Examples: EPI-*DERMIS*, *derma*titis, pachy*derm*
gnosis (knowledge) Greek — Examples: PRO*GNOSIS*, a*gnos*tic, pro*gnos*ticate
gnomon (interpreter) Greek — Examples: PHYSIO*GNOMY*, *gnomon*

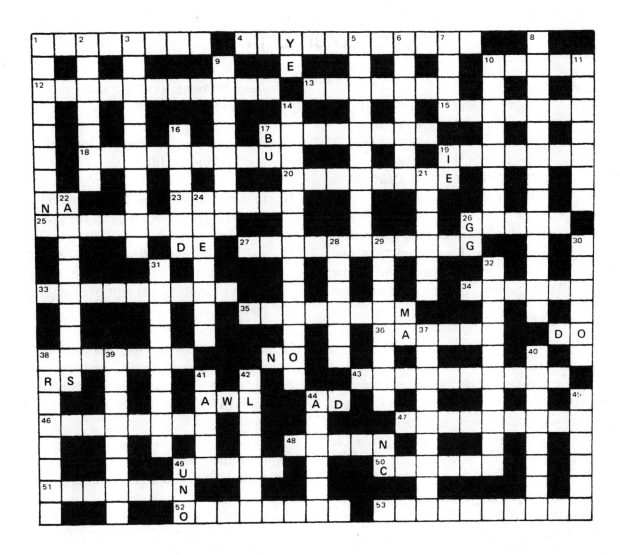

ACROSS

1. a feebleminded person
4. the face, especially as it reveals character
10. a narrow inlet of the sea
12. bulging outward
13. an intimate and exclusive group of followers
15. an agent of revenge or retribution (5)
17. happening every two years
18. so fine as to be transparent; sheer
19. the role of a naive girl in a play
20. under a vow to remain unmarried
23. slow-witted; stupid
25. a recessed door or window opening
26. extremely cold; icy
27. unduly confident
33. the outermost layer of the skin
34. a whirlpool or tornado
35. the belief that events are not under man's own control
36. a small bag filled with perfumed powder
38. dazzlingly bright; radiant
43. to proclaim officially
46. speed; quickness
47. formed of separate parts
48. an offspring, particularly one of wealthy or important parents (8)
49. a government edict or decree
50. a private meeting to make political plans
51. full of self-importance; pompous
52. no longer in style; outdated (5)
53. a friendly or good-humored remark

DOWN

1. to beg earnestly and persistently
2. a hackneyed expression
3. a hard-shelled sea creature
5. outwardly apparent; intended for display
6. a state of perfect blessedness (10)
7. a person's bearing or manner
8. relationship by blood; kinship
9. to season by steeping in a prepared solution
10. to treat with fumes so as to destroy pests
11. to cut into in order to examine
14. intermarriage between persons of different races
16. a winding-sheet for a dead body
21. a tax on imported goods
22. without definite form; shapeless
24. shortness of duration or extent
28. to indulge oneself to excess
29. a representative or agent (15)
30. a caretaker of a church
31. a prediction of the course of a disease
32. touching upon; adjoining
37. self-control; calmness of mind
38. to bear fruit
39. to bring into being; to produce
40. shrill and discordant
41. an Eskimo canoe with a covered top
42. wreckage floating on the sea (13)
44. to come as a natural result
45. people of high social standing in the community

Chapter Eight

Word List 22

ABATTOIR	DICHOTOMY	REPARTEE
ABUT	FRANGIBLE	ROTUND
AGGRIEVED	IMBUE	SEBACEOUS
ASPERSION	MILLENNIUM	SUNDRY
CARDIAC	PACHYDERM	TERMAGANT
DECANT	PREROGATIVE	

Look up the words above in your dictionary. Note that many of them have more than one meaning. When you feel that you know *all* the meanings of *all* the words, go on to the exercises below.

EXERCISE 22A

From the four choices following each phrase or sentence you are to circle the letter preceding the one that is closest in meaning to the italicized word. Where the same word appears more than once, you should note that it is being used in different senses.

1. a large *abattoir* (a) pigsty (b) stable (c) slaughterhouse (d) horse box

2. to *abut* (a) adjoin (b) object (c) surround (d) break up

3. to be *aggrieved* (a) hardened (b) wounded (c) terrified (d) offended

4. to resent his *aspersion* (a) interfering manner (b) remarkable success (c) slanderous remark (d) patronizing offer

5. *cardiac* disorders (a) brain (b) kidney (c) heart (d) lung

6. to *decant* the liquid (a) measure (b) pour (c) stir (d) evaporate

7. a sharp *dichotomy* (a) knife used for preparing microscopic specimens (b) division into two parts (c) exchange of words (d) downward curve on a graph

8. *frangible* bones (a) light and strong (b) easily-broken (c) ancient (d) white

9. to *imbue* with courage (a) conduct oneself (b) resist (c) die (d) fill

10. to last a *millennium* (a) thousand years (b) hundred years (c) ten years (d) year and a day.

11. waiting for the *millennium* (a) year 2000 (b) total destruction of the earth (c) period of perfect happiness (d) visit of beings from other planets

12. a large *pachyderm* (a) sea-dwelling mammal such as the whale (b) scale-covered animal such as a lizard (c) horned animal such as the cow (d) thick-skinned animal such as the elephant

13. It is their *prerogative.* (a) right (b) responsibility (c) decision (d) fault

14. amused by her *repartee* (a) practical joke (b) quick-witted reply (c) clever impersonation (d) surprised expression

15. a *rotund* form (a) towering (b) dim (c) round (d) rotating

16. *sebaceous* substances (a) liquid (b) salty (c) acid (d) fatty

17. *sundry* promises (a) unspoken (b) various (c) sacred (d) broken

18. She is a *termagant.* (a) person authorized to act for others (b) quarrelsome woman (c) person suffering from a fatal disease (d) woman sentenced to jail

Check your answers against the correct ones given on the next page. The answers are not in order; this is to prevent your eye from catching sight of the correct answers before you have had a chance to do the exercise on your own.

8b. 3d. 14b. 17b. 15c. 13a. 2a. 11c. 6b. 4c. 1c. 12d. 10a. 18b. 16d. 9d. 7b. 5c.

Look up in your dictionary all the words for which you gave incorrect answers. Only when you have done this should you go on to the next exercise.

EXERCISE 22B

Each word in Word List 22 is used several times in the sentences below to illustrate different meanings or usage. One of the sentences for each word uses the italicized word incorrectly. You are to circle the letter preceding that sentence.

1. (a) All slaughtering in this *abattoir* is done under government supervision. (b) He killed the animal with a single stroke of his *abattoir*. (c) The animals are stunned on entering the *abattoir* and are then slaughtered.

2. (a) She was going to *abut*, but she swallowed her objection and sat down. (b) He wants to buy the land that *abuts* on the highway. (c) The two farms *abut* each other, but one has fertile soil and the other is barren.

3. (a) You have *aggrieved* me greatly by your attitude. (b) The *aggrieved* party has the right to take the case to court. (c) We *aggrieved* for the loss of our loved ones. (d) We felt quite *aggrieved* at not being invited.

4. (a) You should not cast *aspersions* on her character because you do not have all the facts in the case. (b) I resent the *aspersion* contained in your remarks, and I demand an apology. (c) He made a vague *aspersion* to the money he owed me but then dropped the subject.

5. (a) The first *cardiac* patient to receive a new heart was a resident of Capetown. (b) The *cardiac* muscles are very strong since they pump blood to all parts of the body. (c) Doctors removed the diseased portion of his *cardiac* in a two-hour operation today. (d) A *cardiac* arrest is a temporary or permanent stopping of the heart.

6. (a) The roof was *decanted* at an alarming angle. (b) She *decanted* the wine with care so as not to disturb the sediment at the bottom. (c) The wine was poured from beautiful crystal *decanters*.

7. (a) The novel clearly reveals the *dichotomy* between good and evil in this character. (b) We were in a real *dichotomy*, unable to choose between the two equally-attractive alternatives. (c) The animal world is *dichotomized* into vertebrates and invertebrates. (d) In distinguishing between theory and practice, we introduce a necessary *dichotomy*.

8. (a) *Frangible* bullets, used in firing practice, break up on contact with the target and do not penetrate. (b) The *frangible* odors coming from the kitchen made our mouths water. (c) The tea service is very attractive, but is so *frangible* that it is rarely used.

9. (a) Abraham Lincoln was *imbued* with a deep desire to preserve the Republic. (b) The students are *imbued* with a deep commitment to science. (c) We were *imbued* with enthusiasm after our unexpected victory. (d) We *imbued* our glasses and drank a toast to the bride and groom.

10. (a) Their ninety-foot yacht must have cost them a *millennium*. (b) Instead of sitting around waiting for the *millennium*, we should be working to improve conditions here and now. (c) These records go back many *millenia* to the beginnings of recorded history. (d) The *millennium* mentioned in the Book of Revelation is the thousand years of Christ's reign on earth.

11. (a) The zoo has an elephant, a hippopotamus, and several other *pachyderms*. (b) He is extremely *pachyderm*, and nothing you say to him seems to bother him. (c) She was a skilled elephant-trainer and could make the *pachyderms* under her command do almost anything.

12. (a) He was in an extremely *prerogative* mood, so I decided to keep out of his way. (b)

It was the *prerogative* of the gentry to pursue the fox regardless of whose property was invaded. (c) It is the governor's *prerogative* to commute a sentence of death.

13. (a) Her skill at *repartee* is such that few will debate with her. (b) He would *repartee* every remark that was made, and that soon grew tiresome. (c) The speaker won applause from the audience for her *repartee* directed at the heckler. (d) Beneath the brilliant *repartee* of the play is an underlying seriousness.

14. (a) A chubby faced, *rotund* little man came to the door. (b) The *rotundity* of her form was due entirely to her habit of overeating. (c) The wheels were *rotunding* at different speeds. (d) In rolling, *rotund* phrases the stirring message was delivered to the nation.

15. (a) He gave a *sebaceous* smile as he welcomed us to the inn. (b) Soap is made from a mixture of alkalis and various *sebaceous* substances. (c) The *sebaceous* glands secrete oil to lubricate the skin.

16. (a) There have been *sundry* items in the newspapers regarding the affair. (b) She invited all and *sundry* to the party. (c) With a mighty effort Samson was able to *sundry* the chains that bound him.

17. (a) During the month they were on the island, the two castaways lived on *termagant* eggs and whatever fish they were able to catch. (b) After six months of marriage, he felt he was married to a *termagant*. (c) Their marriage was wrecked by the meddling of his *termagant* mother.

EXERCISE 22C

	Latin	Greek
1	uni-	mono-
2	duo-, bi-	di-
3	tri-	tri-
4	quad-	tetra-
5	quin-	penta-

6	sex-	hexa-
7	sept-	hepta-
8	octo-	octa-
9	non-/nov-	ennea-
10	dec-	deca-
100	cent-	hecto-
1,000	milli-	kilo-

A number of English words are based on Latin and Greek numbers. Using the above table, which gives the principal number roots of both languages, complete the sentences below.

1. A heptagon has . . . . sides.

2. A . . . . is a period of 1,000 years.

3. According to the Roman calendar, September was the . . . . month.

4. A tricycle has . . . . wheels.

5. An actor who plays two separate parts in a play is said to have a . . . . role.

6. An octopus has . . . . tentacles.

7. The Pentagon is a . . . . sided building in Washington that houses the Defense Department.

8. A Catholic . . . . is a nine-day period of prayer.

9. A . . . . person is able to speak two languages.

10. To quadruple one's money is to increase it . . . . fold.

11. The . . . . is a mythical horse-like creature with a single horn.

12. A kilogram is equal to . . . . grams.

13. A tetrahedron is a . . . . -sided solid figure.

14. A decade is a period of . . . . years.

15. . . . . are five babies born to one mother at the same time.

16. A sextet is a musical group comprised of . . . . musicians.

17. A hexameter is a line of verse containing . . . . metrical feet.

18. There are . . . . centimeters to a meter.

19. A . . . . is an eyeglass for one eye.

20. The tenth month of the Roman calendar was . . . .

WORDLY WISE 22

A MILLENNIUM (plural *millennia* or *millenniums*) is a period of 1,000 years. When we speak of "the millennium," we have reference to the anticipated reign of Christ on earth for 1,000 years as mentioned in the Book of Revelation; hence, *millennium* has come to mean any period of perfect blessedness and peace.

PACHYDERM, strictly speaking, refers generally to certain thick-skinned mammals, such as the elephant, the hippopotamus, the rhinocerous, the tapir, the horse, and the pig. In actual usage it has come to be synonymous with *elephant* (The pachyderms at the circus link trunks to tails and form a circle in the ring).

Word List 23

ABSTRUSE	GHETTO	RESURRECT
ANTIQUARY	MADRIGAL	RUDIMENTARY
AUSPICES	NONPAREIL	SOLECISM
CONGRUENCE	OCCIDENT	SURCEASE
DEWLAP	PANDEMIC	VENERATE
DISHABILLE	QUIZZICAL	

Look up the words above in your dictionary. Note that many of them have more than one meaning. When you feel that you know *all* the meanings of *all* the words, go on to the exercises below.

EXERCISE 23A

From the four choices following each phrase or sentence, you are to circle the letter preceding the one that is closest in meaning to the italicized word. Where the same word appears more than once, you should note that it is being used in different senses.

1. *abstruse* writings (a) collected (b) hard to understand (c) childishly simple (d) by a single author

2. He is an *antiquary*. (a) person of great age (b) maker of high-quality furniture (c) person with old-fashioned ideas (d) collector of relics of the past

3. under the *auspices* of someone (a) influence (b) control (c) patronage (d) care

4. the *congruence* of the parts (a) rotation (b) fitting together (c) common area (d) common center

5. a cow's *dewlap* (a) tuft at the end of the tail (b) drinking place (c) fold of skin under the neck (d) block of salt used for licking

6. a state of *dishabille* (a) uncertainty (b) acute embarrassment (c) being regarded with suspicion (d) being partially dressed

7. a large *ghetto* (a) sheltered place resembling a cave (b) body of water located deep underground (c) run-down and overcrowded apartment house (d) section of a city where minorities live because of economic or social pressure

8. a fine *madrigal* (a) lutelike instrument (b) song for several voices (c) woven tapestry showing hunting scenes (d) Spanish-lace shawl

9. She is the *nonpareil*. (a) ringleader (b) one who always takes the blame (c) one whose greatness is unequaled (d) one who always ends up paying

10. a trip to the *Occident* (a) polar regions (b) Western countries (c) Eastern countries (d) equatorial regions

11. *pandemic* diseases (a) widespread (b) incurable (c) mental (d) childhood

12. a *quizzical* look (a) humorously-questioning (b) deeply-perceptive (c) sadly-disillusioned (d) coldly-disinterested

13. to *resurrect* someone (a) publicly humiliate (b) pay off one's debt to (c) restore life to (d) overthrow

14. to *resurrect* a custom (a) mock (b) discard (c) blindly accept (d) bring back

15. *rudimentary* skills (a) necessary (b) undeveloped (c) sophisticated (d) artistic

16. guilty of a *solecism* (a) petty crime (b) selfish act (c) serious crime (d) speech error

17. *surcease* of pain (a) patient bearing (b) increase (c) stopping (d) beginning

18. to *venerate* someone (a) deeply distrust (b) deeply respect (c) deeply dislike (d) look down upon

Check your answers against the correct ones given below. The answers are not in order; this is to prevent your eye from catching sight of the correct answers before you have had a chance to do the exercise on your own.

7d. 10b. 5c. 11a. 17c. 14d. 2d. 12a. 9c. 16d. 1b. 13c. 3c. 8b. 15b. 6d. 4b. 18b.

Look up in your dictionary all the words for which you gave incorrect answers. Only when you have done this should you go on to the next exercise.

EXERCISE 23B

Each word in Word List 23 is used several times in the sentences below to illustrate different meanings or usage. One of the sentences for each word uses the italicized word incorrectly. You are to circle the letter preceding that sentence.

1. (a) He has studied law in the *abstruse* but has no actual legal experience. (b) The mathematics of space travel is too *abstruse* for the ordinary person to understand. (c) Her findings are expressed so *abstrusely* that only a handful of her colleagues can understand them.

2. (a) A magazine for *antiquaries* would deal with ancient coins, manuscripts, weapons, and other relics. (b) His *antiquarian* studies led him into the field of ancient languages. (c) These are objects of great *antiquary* from ancient Crete.

3. (a) The affair is being conducted under the *auspices* of the mayor's office. (b) She has the support of many of the most important *auspices* in town. (c) A small force under the *auspices* of the United Nations will patrol the disputed area.

4. (a) The *congruence* of the two triangles can easily be demonstrated. (b) His theory is *congruent* with the facts so far as they are known. (c) The town grew up at the *congruence* of the two rivers.

5. (a) The animals were *dewlapping* the grass to satisfy their thirsts. (b) Cows and other bovine animals have *dewlaps*, loose folds of skin under the neck. (c) He was a grossly fat man with pendulous *dewlaps* which shook when he talked.

6. (a) They affected not to notice the *dishabille* of the woman and apologized for disturbing

her. (b) His state of *dishabille* indicated he had been about to retire for the night. (c) Her room is always in a state of *dishabille*, but she refuses to keep it tidy.

7. (a) Thousands of Jewish immigrants from the *ghettoes* of Europe poured into New York. (b) The *ghetto* problem of our large cities has not been tackled on any large scale. (c) The *ghetto* had three rooms and rented for sixty dollars a week. (d) It is not easy to break out of the great northern *ghettoes* of New York and Chicago.

8. (a) A ransom of ten thousand gold *madrigals* was paid for the return of the king's son. (b) The *madrigal* reached its greatest popularity in the 16th and 17th centuries. (c) They sang the *madrigal* with great feeling.

9. (a) They drank a toast to Bob Fitzsimmons, the *nonpareil* of prizefighters. (b) The greatest beauty of them all, the *nonpareil*, was the immortal Helen of Troy. (c) Few can equal and none can *nonpareil* her greatness. (d) To listen to her husband, you would think she was the very *nonpareil* of wifely devotion.

10. (a) *Occidental* culture differs strikingly from that of Asia. (b) She spoke *Occidental* with just a trace of an accent. (c) The average *Occidental* regards Indian music as so much noise. (d) Trade between Afro-Asian countries and the *Occident* is increasing rapidly.

11. (a) Typhoid, once *pandemic* in Europe, has been largely eliminated. (b) *Pandemic* broke out in the theatre when someone yelled "Fire!" (c) Terror was *pandemic* as rumors of an invasion from outer space spread quickly. (d) A *pandemic* is an epidemic of unusual severity and extent.

12. (a) He looked *quizzically* at me when I denied all knowledge of the affair. (b) The detective's *quizzical* manner concealed a mind that was very sharp indeed. (c) The professor's *quizzical*

approach to world problems left many students questioning his seriousness. (d) "This is not a *quizzical* matter," she said angrily. "I suggest you take it seriously."

13. (a) It is hopeless to try to *resurrect* these old customs that have fallen into disuse. (b) Some of the songs she sang were *resurrected* from shows of forty years ago and more. (c) The *Resurrection* of Christ following His death three days before is one of the tenets of Christianity. (d) The officers were charged with armed *resurrection* against the ruler and were executed.

14. (a) The children receive a *rudimentary* education that barely fits them for the complexities of modern life. (b) A *rudimentary* schoolhouse was built out of discarded pieces of lumber. (c) A tadpole has *rudimentary* legs which become fully developed in the frog. (d) The solution to the problem is so *rudimentary* I'm surprised you haven't found it yet.

15. (a) His mood of *solecism* is the result of a desire to avoid contact with strangers. (b) The frequent *solecisms* in his speech betrayed his lack of formal education. (c) We can correct the *solecism* in "She was quite independent on them" by replacing "on" with "of."

16. (a) There were no drugs available to give her *surcease* from the pain that racked her body. (b) The explorers were offered a *surcease* of good things to eat by the friendly Indians. (c) In the confines of the monastery he will find *surcease* from worldly cares.

17. (a) In most Asian countries, persons are taught to *venerate* their ancestors. (b) Artists were held in tremendous *veneration* during this period. (c) The cardinal, very wise, very dignified, was a truly *venerable* figure. (d) Bobby *venerated* his anger on his sister by smashing her doll's house.

EXERCISE 23C

Complete the following analogies by underlining the numbered pair of words which are related to each other in the same way as the first pair are related.

1. Japan:Orient:: (1) Tokyo:Occident (2) Tokyo: Japan (3) Paris:France (4) France:Occident (5) Paris:Occident

2. millenium:decade:: (1) 100:10 (2) century:year (3) decade:year (4) century:decade (5) 10:1

3. biennial:biannual:: (1) 2:½ (2) day:night (3) decant:decent (4) yearly:monthly (5) ¼:½

4. obtuse:acute:: (1) ∠:∟ (2) ∟:∟ (3) ∠:∟ (4) ∟:∠ (5) ∟:∠

5. imbecile:intelligence:: (1) fire:warmth (2) invalid:health (3) coward:fear (4) money:wealth

6. amorphous:shape:: (1) inanimate:life (2) huge:size (3) phlegmatic:dull (4) humorous:comedy (5) verdant:green

7. crab:crustacean:: (1) turtle:carapace (2) kangaroo:pouch (3) pouch:shell (4) kangaroo:marsupial (5) crustacean:marsupial

8. wolf:lupine:: (1) cat:dog (2) dog:wolf (3) feline:canine (4) dog:canine (5) wild:tame

WORDLY WISE 23

AUSPICES is a plural noun; the singular form *auspice* is correct and may be used interchangeably with *auspices*. Note that the plural form is more commonly used.

DISHABILLE, a French word, is pronounced *dis-ə-BEEL*.

The plural of GHETTO is *ghettoes* or *ghettos*.

The people of Soloi, a Greek colonial city, are now remembered chiefly for their ignorance of proper Greek. Their contemporaries coined the word *soloikizein* ("to speak like a citizen of Soloi; to speak incorrectly") and from it is derived SOLECISM, meaning "a grammatical blunder," "something deviating from the proper or accepted order," and "a breach of etiquette."

Etymology

Study the roots given below together with the English words derived from them. Capitalized words are those given in the Word List. You should look up in a dictionary any words that are unfamiliar to you.

Roots: *antiquus* (ancient) Latin — Examples: ANTIQUARY, *antique, antiqu*ated

auspicium (omen) Latin — Examples: AUSPICES, *auspic*ious

resurgere (rise again) Latin — Examples: RESURRECT, *resurg*ence

---

Word List 24

ACRONYM	MARQUETRY	RIFT
ARCHETYPE	NOTARY	RUMINATE
CADENCE	OBLATE	STRATAGEM
CONSUMMATE	ORDINAL	TEMPERAMENT
DIADEM	PLACATE	VERTIGO
IMBROGLIO	REGENERATION	

Look up the words above in your dictionary. Note that many of them have more than one meaning. When you feel that you know *all* the meanings of *all* the words, go on to the exercises below.

EXERCISE 24A

From the four choices following each phrase or sentence, you are to circle the letter preceding the one that is closest in meaning to the italicized word. Where the same word appears more than once, you should note that it is being used in different senses.

1. to devise an *acronym* (a) word reading the same spelled backward (b) word made by rearranging its letters (c) word made from the initial letters of other words (d) word used to unlock a coded message

2. an *archetype* in literature (a) particular style (b) body of stories (c) new approach (d) original model

3. a regular *cadence* (a) foot soldier (b) monetary payment (c) assumed obligation (d) rhythmic beat

4. to *consummate* the deal (a) call off (b) complete (c) investigate (d) delay

5. a *consummate* design (a) symmetrical (b) secret (c) unfinished (d) perfect

6. a jewelled *diadem* (a) cross (b) brooch (c) crown (d) gown

7. involved in an *imbroglio* (a) business deal (b) confused situation (c) diplomatic mission (d) secret alliance

8. a fine piece of *marquetry* (a) artwork made from pieces of scrap metal (b) writing that mocks human nature (c) decorative inlaid woodwork (d) business maneuvering

9. a *notary* public (a) official able to certify documents (b) official able to perform marriages (c) building belonging to the federal government (d) piece of land belonging to the people

10. an *oblate* spheroid (a) peffectly round (b) revolving (c) elongated at the poles (d) flattened at the poles

11. *ordinal* numbers (a) expressing negative quantities (b) expressing order in a series (c) expressing fractional quantities (d) expressing positive quantities

12. to *placate* someone (a) annoy (b) announce (c) pacify (d) oppose

13. a person's *regeneration* (a) line of descendents (b) spiritual rebirth (c) line of ancestors (d) second childhood

14. *regeneration* of an organ (a) renewal (b) sudden loss (c) evolutionary development (d) withering away

15. a *rift* in the earth's surface (a) weakness (b) crack (c) hole (d) layer of rock

16. Cows *ruminate.* (a) live in herds (b) moo (c) produce milk (d) chew the cud

17. to *ruminate* (a) regret (b) meditate (c) overeat (d) grow angry

18. a clever *stratagem* (a) scheme (b) remark (c) general (d) solution

19. a violent *temperament* (a) outburst of rage (b) customary frame of mind (c) clash between armies (d) swing from one level to another

20. suffering from *vertigo* (a) poor eyesight (b) poor hearing (c) dizziness (d) muscular aches

Check your answers against the correct ones given below. The answers are not in order; this is to prevent your eye from catching sight of the correct answers before you have had a chance to do the exercise on your own.

4b. 1c. 18a. 16d. 6c. 15b. 8c. 3d. 13b. 19b. 14a. 2d. 20c. 12c. 9a. 7b. 10d. 5d. 11b. 17b.

Look up in your dictionary all the words for which you gave incorrect answers. Only when you have done this should you go on to the next exercise.

EXERCISE 24B

Each word in Word List 24 is used several times in the sentences below to illustrate different meanings or usage. One of the sentences for each word uses the italicized word incorrectly. You are to circle the letter preceding that sentence.

1. (a) "Radar" is an *acronym* formed from (ra)dio (d)etecting (a)nd (r)anging. (b) "Madam, I'm Adam" is an *acronym* because it reads the same forward or backward.

2. (a) I *archetyped* her as untrustworthy as soon as I saw her. (b) Moses is an *archetypal* figure in Judeo-Christian thought. (c) In Don Quixote we have the *archetype* of the fumbling, well-meaning idealist. (d) The United States constitution is the *archetype* of those newly written by emerging nations.

3. (a) The poem imitates the *cadence* of marching feet. (b) In stately, *cadenced* verse

93

he tells of the battle between Greeks and Trojans. (c) The *cadence* of the country-woman's speech was quite different from that of city folk. (d) The soldiers formed a solid *cadence* and marched across the square.

4. (a) This carving is a work of *consummate* artistry. (b) This was the *consummation* of all my hopes. (c) The deal was *consummated* with nothing more formal than a handshake. (d) For the benefit of those who arrived late I will *consummate* what I said earlier.

5. (a) The largest *diadem* in the crown was a ruby as large as a pigeon's egg. (b) The *diadem*, sparkling with precious stones, was placed on the queen's head. (c) The *diadem* monkey gets its name from the crown-like markings on its head.

6. (a) The *imbroglio* was caused by three nations claiming the disputed territory. (b) The author got into a hopeless *imbroglio* with her publisher over paperback and screen rights to her book. (c) He is never happier than when about to *imbroglio* himself in someone else's affairs. (d) Her attempts to settle the *imbroglio* seem only to have aggravated it.

7. (a) The king touched his shoulder with the sword, admitting him into the ranks of the *marquetry*. (b) Skillful *marquetry* requires that the inlaid pieces of wood fit together perfectly. (c) The next item to be sold was a low table decorated with some fine *marquetry*.

8. (a) The document is valueless until it has been *notarized*. (b) A *notary* public is authorized to certify deeds and other legal documents. (c) He is an infamous person, and a certain amount of *notary* attaches to anyone seen associating with him.

9. (a) The earth is not a perfect sphere but rather an *oblate* spheroid. (b) She *oblated* the piece of clay, flattening it into a thick disk.

10. (a) One, two, three are cardinal numbers; first, second, third are *ordinal* numbers. (b) The chief of the seven *ordinal* virtues are faith, hope, and charity.

11. (a) His offer to pay for the damage *placated* the owner of the car he had rammed. (b) These government measures will be quite ineffective and have been promised merely to *placate* the public. (c) "I'm sorry if I offended you with my remark," she said *placatingly*. (d) His offer to help is a *placate* designed to soothe and is not sincerely given.

12. (a) They attribute their *regeneration* to the missionary work of the priests. (b) A lizard that loses its tail is able to *regenerate* a new one. (c) This land has been in her family for many *regenerations*. (d) A fine example has greater *regenerative* effect on people than all the sermons in the world.

13. (a) The clouds *rifted* and the sun broke through. (b) He was *rift* of everything he possessed when his house burned down. (c) The *rift* runs for hundreds of miles and is believed to have been caused by a fault in the earth's crust. (d) The two cousins deplored the *rift* that set them apart, but neither made any attempt to heal it.

14. (a) A cow *ruminates* so that the grass it eats may be digested more easily. (b) He puffed at his pipe and *ruminated* for a while before replying. (c) She will *ruminate* the day that she crossed my path. (d) The most common of the *ruminants,* or cud-chewing animals, is the cow.

15. (a) He was able to *stratagem* the enemy into leaving his flanks unprotected. (b) The general relied on the superiority of his firepower and had no need to resort to *stratagem*. (c) We must guard against the *stratagems* of the enemy. (d) Her offer to buy was a *stratagem* to find out who else was interested in the property.

16. (a) She has the soul of a poet joined to the *temperament* of a woman of business. (b) His *temperament* is uncertain early in the morning, so be careful what you say to him. (c) These horses are very *temperamental*; one never knows what they will do next. (d) She advocates *temperament* in the partaking of alcoholic beverages.

17. (a) He had an acute attack of *vertigo* and sat down quickly lest he fall. (b) *Vertigo* is commonly experienced when people look at the ground from a great height. (c) In winning the Nobel prize, he has reached the very *vertigo* of success.

EXERCISE 24C

This exercise combines synonyms and antonyms. You are to underline the word which is *either* most similar in meaning *or* most nearly opposite in meaning to the capitalized word. Underline only one word for each question after deciding that it is either an antonym or a synonym, and write A (for antonym) or S (for synonym) after the capitalized word. Allow 15 minutes only for this test. If you cannot answer a question, go on to the next without delay. If you have time left over at the end, go back and try to fill in unanswered questions.

26 or over correct:	excellent
22 to 25 correct:	good
21 or under correct:	thorough review of A exercises indicated

1. RIGHT . . . .
   prerogative tariff maxim opprobrium dichotomy

2. MEDITATE . . . .
   ruminate resurrect venerate fructify dote

3. AGREEMENT . . . .
   cornucopia congruence acronym solecism surcease

4. GENUINE . . . .
   ordinal frangible gelid ersatz beatific

5. PLEASED . . . .
   strident amorphous aggrieved refractory disjointed

6. TERSE . . . .
   verbose cardiac composite effete agenda

7. SCHEME . . . .
   pachyderm vertigo stratagem sachet blandishment

8. FRAGILE . . . .
   frangible abstruse obtuse clandestine felicitous

9. PRAISE . . . .
   marquetry upbraid miscegenation temporize protocol

10. PATRONAGE . . . .
    congruence antiquary aspersion auspices prerogative

11. COMPLETE . . . .
    pandemic importune consummate iridescent educe

12. SIMPLE . . . .
    sebaceous abstruse nonpareil quizzical meretricious

13. DIZZINESS . . . .
    dipsomania innuendo claustrophobia turpitude vertigo

14. ROUND . . . .
    fustian consummate notary opulent rotund

15. ADJOIN . . . .
    imbue accrue leaven abut dissemble

16. POUR . . . .
    decant placate accrue meander recant

17. FATTY . . . .
    wallow sebaceous rudimentary overweening merino

18. SPLIT . . . .
brevity decant rift coterie misdemeanor

19. ANGER . . . .
obviate tonsure dishabille nullify placate

20. SHORTAGE . . . .
plethora abattoir stratagem celerity panegyric

21. VARIOUS . . . .
oblate hirsute unwonted sundry sapient

22. CESSATION . . . .
archetype embrasure prognosis surcease effrontery

23. SLAUGHTERHOUSE . . . .
caucus ghetto abattoir imbroglio termagant

24. WIDESPREAD . . . .
verbose pandemic diaphanous rotund didactic

25. SHREW . . . .
temperament dewlap crustacean vernacular termagant

26. CROWN . . . .
sachet repartee millenium diadem carapace

27. SCORN . . . .
imbue abut venerate regeneration ruminate

28. COMPLEX . . . .
phlegmatic anterior verbose rudimentary vibrant

29. RENEWAL . . . .
depredation cadence doctrine refractory regeneration

30. DIVISION . . . .
dichotomy archetype embrasure epidermis durance

WORDLY WISE 24

CONSUMMATE as a verb is pronounced *KON-sum-ate*; as an adjective it is pronounced *kən-SUM-it*.

IMBROGLIO is pronounced *im-BROLE-yo*.

The *cardinal* numbers (one, two, three, etc.) are those used in counting and for expressions of quantity; the ORDINAL numbers (first, second, third, etc.) express *order* in a series. *Cardinal* has an additional, adjectival meaning: "chief; most important" (the cardinal virtues).

Etymology

Study the roots and prefix given below together with the English words derived from them. Capitalized words are those given in the Word List. You should look up in a dictionary any words that are unfamiliar to you.

Prefix: (review) *re-* (again) Latin — Examples: REGENERATION, *re*new

Roots: *genus, genera* (birth, race) Latin — Examples: RE*GENERA*TION, *genera*tion, *gener*ic

vertere (turn) Latin — Examples: VER*T*IGO, re*vert*, intro*vert*

onyma (name) Greek — Examples: ACR*ONYM*, pseud*onym*, an*onym*ous

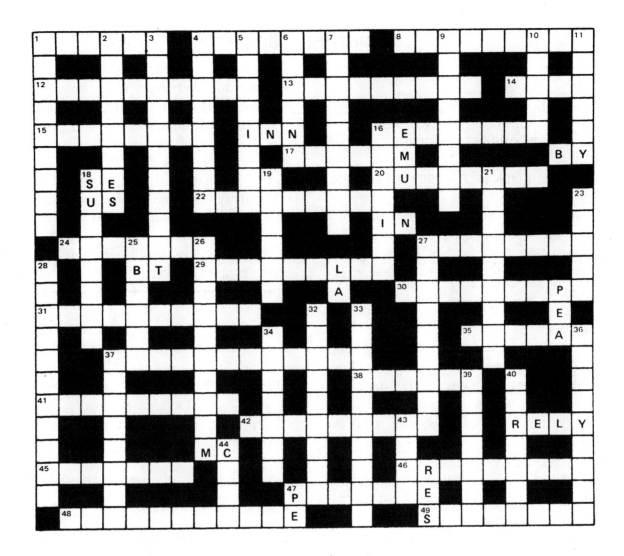

ACROSS

1. to pour gently
4. hard to understand
8. a damaging or disparaging remark
12. to bring to completion
13. a quarrelsome, scolding woman
14. to touch at one end; to adjoin
15. Europe and the Western hemisphere
16. to regard with deep respect; to revere
17. a jewelled or ornamented headband; a crown
20. to reflect on; to meditate
22. to bring back to life
24. a word formed from the first letters of other words
27. a song with parts for several voices
29. a confused or complicated situation
30. an original pattern or model
31. carelessly dressed; partially undressed
35. a fold of skin under the neck
37. spiritual rebirth; renewal
38. a section of a city where a minority is forced to live
41. one whose greatness is unequalled
42. one who collects or studies relics of the past
45. a platform for speechmaking (4)
46. easily broken
47. to keep from being angry; to soothe
48. a right attached to an office or position
49. a mistake in speech or writing

DOWN

1. a division into two parts
2. patronage; guidance
3. frame of mind; disposition
4. a slaughterhouse
5. seemingly true but actually false (5)
6. full and round
7. a clever trick or scheme
9. affecting many people; widespread
10. to fill; to saturate, as with a feeling of emotion
11. an official able to certify documents
16. a feeling of dizziness
18. a stopping or cessation
19. various; miscellaneous
21. having a grievance; offended
23. a noisy, confused fight or brawl (12)
25. flattened at the poles
26. a period of 1,000 years
27. decorative, inlaid woodwork
28. not fully developed
32. humorously questioning
33. correspondence or agreement of parts
34. a rhythmic flow or sequence
36. a large, thick-skinned animal, as the elephant
37. a quick, witty reply
39. expressing order in a series
40. of or relating to the heart
43. an opening caused by splitting
44. a small, pouch-like growth (14)

Chapter Nine

Word List 25

ANALGESIC	ECOLOGY	MESMERIZE
ATTRITION	ENCLAVE	NOMINEE
CEREBRAL	EPITOME	QUEUE
CONTUMELY	GRANDIOSE	RISQUÉ
DEMULCENT	INALIENABLE	SUBTERRANEAN

Look up the words above in your dictionary. Note that many of them have more than one meaning. When you feel that you know *all* the meanings of *all* the words, go on to the exercises below.

EXERCISE 25A

From the four choices following each phrase or sentence, you are to circle the letter preceding the one that is closest in meaning to the italicized word. Where the same word appears more than once, you should note that it is being used in different senses.

1. a powerful *analgesic* (a) pain-killing drug (b) high explosive (c) scene in a play or story (d) wartime ally

2. to cause *attrition* (a) a gradual increase in strength (b) a gradual wearing down (c) a sudden collapse (d) a sudden increase

3. *cerebral* palsy (a) lung (b) brain (c) muscle (d) stomach

4. a *cerebral* poet (a) lyric (b) intellectual (c) puritanical (d) imaginative

5. "the proud man's *contumely*" (a) fine clothes (b) boastful manner (c) unwillingness to admit mistakes (d) insulting language

6. a *demulcent* preparation (a) soothing (b) adhesive (c) hardening (d) liquid

7. a knowledge of *ecology* (a) the study of the growing of garden plants (b) the study of the earth's atmosphere (c) the study of the re-lationship between living things and their environment (d) the study of the selective breeding of animals

8. a small *enclave* (a) private meeting of a political nature (b) area enclosed by foreign territory (c) armed landing behind enemy lines (d) temporary shelter against the elements

9. the *epitome* of excellence (a) direct opposite (b) gradual erosion (c) scornful condemnation (d) ideal expression of

10. *grandiose* schemes (a) petty (b) not quite legal (c) pretentiously exaggerated (d) costly

11. *inalienable* rights (a) that cannot be taken away (b) that cannot be restored once lost (c) that are granted by the federal government (d) that must be seized by the people

12. to *mesmerize* someone (a) soothe (b) startle (c) remind (d) hypnotize

13. to be a *nominee* (a) person using an assumed name (b) representative type (c) person named as a candidate (d) ruler who exercises no real power

14. to join the *queue* (a) circle of admirers (b) line of persons waiting (c) secret organization (d) splinter group within a party

15. a long *queue* (a) pigtail (b) leather whip (c) cowboy's rope (d) burst of applause

16. a *risqué* story (a) stirring (b) lengthy (c) improper (d) vivid

17. *subterranean* streams (a) bridgeable (b) rock-strewn (c) shallow (d) underground

Check your answers against the correct ones given on the next page. The answers are not in order; this is to prevent your eye from catching sight of the correct answers before you have had a chance to do the exercise on your own.

6a. 5d. 4b. 1a. 12d. 10c. 16c. 9d. 7c. 8b. 3b. 14b. 17d. 15a. 13c. 2b. 11a.

Look up in your dictionary all the words for which you gave incorrect answers. Only when you have done this should you go on to the next exercise.

EXERCISE 25B

Each word in Word List 25 is used several times in the sentences below to illustrate different meanings or usage. One of the sentences for each word uses the italicized word incorrectly. You are to circle the letter preceding that sentence.

1. (a) An *analgesic* kills pain without causing loss of consciousness. (b) The *analgesic* properties of aspirin are well known. (c) He is receiving treatment for a painful *analgesia* of the shoulder muscles. (d) Methyl salicylate is a balm that induces *analgesia* when rubbed into the skin.

2. (a) A conflict marked by gradual wearing down of forces on both sides is called a war of *attrition*. (b) The poem deals with the slow *attrition* of the human soul in the modern world. (c) The rate of *attrition* of these machines is increased if they are improperly serviced. (d) The false *attrition* of this story to a presidential aide was due to an unfortunate error.

3. (a) A *cerebral* hemorrhage is caused by a blood vessel bursting in the brain. (b) The leader was a *cerebral* type, always engaging in learned discussions with others. (c) Her *cerebral* was injured when her head struck the dashboard of the car.

4. (a) In his greatest soliloquy, Hamlet refers bitterly to "the proud man's *contumely*." (b) Her *contumely* manner served only to aggravate the problem she was trying to resolve. (c) The book is not a reasoned argument, but a vicious attack, bristling with *contumely*. (d) A candidate for high office must be able to bear the *contumely* of political opponents without complaining.

5. (a) She bowed *demulcently* when she was introduced. (b) The *demulcent* properties of flaxseed make it useful for the relief of sore throats. (c) There are a number of *demulcents* on the market that soothe inflamed mucous membrane.

6. (a) The animals were suffering from *ecology*, so we called in the veterinarian. (b) *Ecology*, a branch of biology, is concerned with the relation between living things and their environment. (c) The wholesale destruction of forest land, without consideration of *ecological* factors, is bound to have disastrous consequences. (d) The *ecology* of the arctic regions is not yet fully understood.

7. (a) Delegates to the convention met in secret *enclave* to choose their candidate. (b) Vatican City is an *enclave* held by the pope, situated within the city of Rome. (c) The areas held by our forces should be defended as *enclaves*, and the enemy allowed to hold the rest of the country.

8. (a) His manner of receiving us was the *epitome* of politeness. (b) Her history of the revolution was a vast *epitome* covering five volumes. (c) We need a leader who *epitomizes* all that is best in us as a nation. (d) In his marine uniform he was the very *epitome* of military tradition.

9. (a) She loves to flash hundred-dollar bills and talk *grandiosely* of her business deals. (b) He wore the fine clothes and had the proud manner of a Spanish *grandiose*. (c) The collapse of her business enterprises failed to halt her *grandiose* schemes for the future.

10. (a) The Declaration of Independence guarantees our *inalienable* right to life, liberty, and

the pursuit of happiness. (b) I am *inalienably* opposed to these measures. (c) These *inalienably*-granted rights are not subject to the whim of any individual ruler.

11. (a) He stared as though *mesmerized* at the message he held in his hand. (b) She had *mesmerized* the message and was able to repeat it word for word. (c) His *mesmeric* power over his followers was due in large measure to his spellbinding voice. (d) She had studied *mesmerism* and was able to put a person into a hypnotic trance at will.

12. (a) The president's *nominee* for the vacancy on the Supreme Court must be approved by the Senate. (b) The Republican Party *nominee* for governor has promised to reduce taxes if elected. (c) Whom will he *nominee* for the post? (d) Academy Award *nominees* are not told ahead of time which of them has won the coveted "Oscar."

13. (a) She offered to *queue* us as to the type of question likely to be asked. (b) We joined the end of the *queue* and waited patiently to be served. (c) The Chinese once wore their hair in *queues*, but this is no longer the custom. (d) It is better to *queue* up at the bus stop than for everyone to try to rush onto the bus at once.

14. (a) Several people in the audience seemed to enjoy the *risqué* stories very much. (b) Deactivating live bombs is *risqué* work that appeals to very few people.

15. *Subterranean* streams abound in these parts because of the limestone hills. (b) Records are stored in vast *subterranean* vaults hundreds of feet below the surface. (c) She spoke English with a slight *subterranean* accent.

EXERCISE 25C

Complete the following words for which prefixes and suffixes have been supplied by filling in the appropriate form of each of the given Greek roots. Give a brief definition of each word in the space provided.

derm(a) (skin)

1. P A C H Y _____ . . . .

. . . .

2. _____ A T O L O G I S T . . . .

. . . .

3. E P I _____ I S . . . .

. . . .

4. _____ A T I T I S . . . .

. . . .

dem(os) (people)

5. _____ C R A C Y . . . .

. . . .

6. E P I _____ I C . . . .

. . . .

7. _____ A G O G U E . . . .

. . . .

8. P A N _____ I C . . . .

. . . .

the(os) (god)

9. _____ O L O G Y . . . .

. . . .

10. A _____ I S T . . . .

. . . .

11. M O N O _____ I S M . . . .

. . . .

12. _____OCRACY . . . .

. . . .

WORDLY WISE 25

Ad- is a prefix meaning "to" and suggests motion or attraction toward something. Like the prefix *com-* (Wordly Wise 17), *ad-* sometimes changes its consonant to blend more readily with the initial sound of a root. *ATTRITION* is made from *ad-* plus a form of the Latin verb *terere* ("to rub"), with the *d* changed to *t* for easier pronunciation. It means "friction," "the act of rubbing together," or "grinding down"; a war of attrition, for example, is one carried on by weakening and wearing down the enemy rather than by fighting major battles. *Affinity* (Word List 11) is also made with *ad-* and means "attraction of one thing for another" or "relationship." Other forms in which *ad-* may occur are *ac-, ag-, al-, an-, ap-, ar-,* and *as-.*

An *ENCLAVE* is an area enclosed by foreign or alien territory; a *conclave* (Word List 12) is a private meeting, specifically a meeting of cardinals to elect a pope. Do not confuse these two terms.

QUEUE is pronounced *KYEW*.

RISQUÉ (pronounced *ris-KAY*) must always be spelled with the accent over the *e*.

Word List 26

ANTEDILUVIAN	ENDEMIC	PRECIPITATE
AVOUCH	FAKIR	QUILL
CHAUVINIST	HABILIMENTS	SONIC
DEBAUCHED	LEVITATION	THRENODY
DISSONANCE	MILLINER	WINSOME
EFFIGY		

Look up the words above in your dictionary. Note that many of them have more than one meaning. When you feel that you know *all* the meanings of *all* the words, go on to the following exercises.

EXERCISE 26A

From the four choices following each phrase or sentence, you are to circle the letter preceding the one that is closest in meaning to the italicized word. Where the same word appears more than once, you should note that it is being used in different senses.

1. *antediluvian* methods (a) old-fashioned (b) well-tried (c) novel (d) futuristic

2. to *avouch* something (a) deny weakly (b) declare positively (c) add to (d) fear

3. He is a *chauvinist*. (a) deeply religious person (b) wickedly deceitful person (c) fanatically patriotic person (d) weakminded person

4. thoroughly *debauched* (a) exhausted (b) disproved (c) cleansed (d) corrupted

5. complete *dissonance* (a) lack of interest (b) range of sounds (c) lack of harmony (d) lack of sound

6. an *effigy* on a coin (a) mint mark (b) date (c) likeness (d) worn area

7. an *effigy* of someone (a) stuffed dummy (b) perfect double (c) enemy (d) friend

8. *endemic* diseases (a) caused by living in the Tropics (b) that respond easily to treatment (c) restricted to a particular area (d) spreading rapidly over wide areas

9. an old *fakir* (a) carnival attendant (b) Mediterranean carpet dealer (c) Muslim holy man (d) doctor lacking proper qualifications

10. a priest's *habiliments* (a) assistants (b) parishioners (c) garb (d) duties

11. the *levitation* of a body (a) mysterious disappearance (b) apparent rotation (c) apparent raising into the air (d) mysterious appearance

12. a visit to the *milliner* (a) seller of flowers (b) seller of flour (c) seller of men's hats (d) seller of women's hats

13. to *precipitate* an event (a) guard against (b) do everything to delay (c) prepare oneself for (d) bring about too soon

14. to *precipitate* a substance (a) chemically combine (b) separate from a liquid (c) determine the constituents of (d) stir vigorously

15. a *precipitate* act (a) rash (b) considered (c) confident (d) timorous

16. a goose *quill* (a) wing (b) feather (c) webbed foot (d) crest

17. a porcupine *quill* (a) feeding spot (b) claw (c) tooth (d) spine

18. to pick up the *quill* (a) book (b) pen (c) cover (d) headdress

19. *sonic* waves (a) sound (b) light (c) radio (d) ocean

20. to compose a *threnody* (a) speech of welcome (b) song of lamentation (c) song of joy (d) speech of farewell

21. a *winsome* manner (a) pleasant (b) crafty (c) gloomy (d) nervous

Check your answers against the correct ones given below. The answers are not in order; this is to prevent your eye from catching sight of the correct answers before you have had a chance to do the exercise on your own.

18b. 4d. 6c. 15a. 8c. 3c. 13d. 19a. 1a. 16b. 9c. 12d. 20b. 2b. 14b. 21a. 17d. 11c. 5c. 10c. 7a.

Look up in your dictionary all the words for which you gave incorrect answers. Only when you have done this should you go on to the next exercise.

EXERCISE 26B

Each word in Word List 26 is used several times in the following sentences to illustrate different meanings or usage. One of the sentences for each word uses the italicized word incorrectly. You are to circle the letter preceding that sentence.

1. (a) The methods being employed were so *antediluvian* that we recommended they be scrapped. (b) *Antediluvian* persons, literally speaking, are those who lived before the time of Noah's Flood. (c) Automobiles of the twenties look positively *antediluvian* compared to today's cars. (d) The presence of *antediluvian* in the earth's rocks indicates the presence of oil.

2. (a) "I didn't touch it," she said *avouchly*. (b) His innocence was *avouched* by both witnesses to the crime. (c) I can *avouch* the accuracy of what she says.

3. (a) Only the *chauvinist* refuses to admit that his country can, on occasion, be wrong. (b) *Chauvinism* is one of the strongest barriers against a strong United Nations. (c) It is *chauvinistic* to deny the rights of other countries in this matter. (d) These people were *chauvinisted* into supporting their country.

4. (a) The emperor Nero was a thoroughly *debauched* person to whom no depraved act was alien. (b) The young woman *debauched* from the coach at the next stop. (c) His *debauched* face was evidence of the depravity of his life. (d) A lax press and a *debauched* legislature led the way for wholesale bribery and corruption.

5. (a) The harmonic flow of the music is jarred by an occasional deliberately *dissonant* passage. (b) The mingling of high tragedy with broad comedy results in a certain overall *dissonance* in the play. (c) Her *dissonant* manner made me suspect that something was troubling her. (d) The *dissonance* of the notes caused the conductor to chide the orchestra.

6. (a) The *effigy* of the empress appeared on every coin of the empire. (b) We will test the *effigy* of their new methods before making up our minds. (c) The football coach was hanged in *effigy* when the team lost 36-0. (d) The Black Prince lies in *effigy* on top of the tomb that contains his remains.

7. (a) The snobbery you refer to is not *endemic* to the upper classes; it is found also among

the lower classes. (b) Malaria is *endemic* to most tropical countries. (c) Marsupials, such as the kangaroo, are *endemic* to Australia. (d) The flu *endemic* spread quickly through the country.

8. (a) The *fakir* is considered a holy man because of his fasting and general abstinence. (b) The *fakirs* of Arab countries depend on the generosity of others for their daily bread. (c) Most of the questions are straightforward, but there is an occasional *fakir* designed to trip you up.

9. (a) The Indians live in small *habiliments* pitched along the banks of the river. (b) A top hat and morning coat were his usual *habiliments* for trips to the races. (c) I could see by his clerical *habiliments* that he was a priest.

10. (a) Few people believe in *levitation*, which is the raising of a body in the air without any form of support. (b) Persons with supernatural powers claim to be able to *levitate* chairs and tables. (c) She *levitated* her arms in a gesture of prayer and sank slowly to her knees.

11. (a) The *millinery* department has a large assortment of hats for women. (b) She made the hat out of a yard of *millinery* and some ribbon. (c) My aunt stopped at the *milliner's* to look at some hats. (d) She is an expert *milliner* and can make an attractive hat out of any old scraps of material.

12. (a) The sudden withdrawal of the drug may *precipitate* a violent reaction. (b) We walked to the edge of the *precipitate* and looked fearfully over the edge. (c) We must not be *precipitate* in offering to help the emerging nations; we should first find out if they need our help. (d) The application of heat will *precipitate* the crystals from the solution.

13. (a) I sharpened the *quill* with my penknife and commenced to write. (b) A porcupine can eject its *quills* with great force into whatever is annoying it. (c) There was a heavy down

quill on the bed to keep the children warm. (d) The large *quills* from the tail or wings were best suited to pen-making.

14. (a) Following the examination, the doctor told the patient that his heart was quite *sonic*. (b) A *sonic* mine is activated by sounds from the ship passing overhead. (c) A *sonic* boom is caused when a plane exceeds the speed of sound and the shock wave thus caused strikes the ground.

15. (a) They fell to the ground in a violent *threnody* of pain, gasping in agony. (b) Numerous *threnodies* were composed on the death of the national leader. (c) The *threnody* laments the passing of all who died in battle.

16. (a) His *winsome* manner and bright smile won him many admirers. (b) She could *winsome* her way into a person's heart with her smile alone. (c) The child smiled *winsomely* at them and wished them good morning.

EXERCISE 26C

In each of the sentences below a word is omitted. From the four words provided, select the one that best completes the sentence. Allow ten minutes for this test. If you cannot answer a question, go on to the next one without delay. If you have time left over at the end, go back and try to fill in unanswered questions.

18 or over correct:	excellent
14 to 17 correct:	good
13 or under correct:	thorough review of A exercises indicated

1. "NATO" is an . . . . for North Atlantic Treaty Organization.
   archetype initial acronym ukase

2. Nuclear energy is being used increasingly to . . . . electricity.
   decant generate placate venerate

3. His voice grew . . . . as he scolded the children for breaking the window.
grandiose strident endemic amorphous

4. The . . . . is good, and the patient should be walking in a few days.
prognosis threnody endemic physiognomy

5. The hero of the novel is a . . . . of several persons known to the author.
coterie consummate contiguous composite

6. By far the commonest . . . . is simple aspirin.
analgesic demulcent solecism pandemic

7. The sturdy country squire was the . . . . of the English gentry.
millennium epitome consummate prerogative

8. . . . . is concerned with the relationship between living things and their environment.
physiognomy genealogy ecology claustrophobia

9. Certain rights are held to be . . . . and are not subject to the whims of government.
inalienable rudimentary pandemic abstruse

10. The . . . . finds it hard to believe that one can criticize one's country and still be patriotic.
antiquary chauvinist ingenue fakir

11. A war of . . . . is one in which heavy casualties are suffered by both sides.
consanguinity miscegenation regeneration attrition

12. Slavery was . . . . to the southern states prior to the Civil War.
epidemic endemic pandemic clairvoyant

13. When a plane exceeds the speed of sound, a . . . . boom is created.
frangible cardiac sonic demulcent

14. Her . . . . schemes for making a fortune have no basis in reality.
protuberant quizzical grandiose beatific

15. Persons looking down from a great height often experience acute . . . .
vertigo panacea innuendo claustrophobia

16. I demand an apology for the . . . . you have cast on my good name.
prognosis tonsure depredation aspersion

17. The earth is an . . . . spheroid.
empyrean obviate anterior oblate

18. The parents have tried to . . . . their children with a deep love of country.
imbue expiate avouch precipitate

19. Most of our large cities have . . . . areas where living standards leave much to be desired.
ersatz ghetto trenchant subterranean

20. Too hasty action on our part could . . . . a serious crisis.
placate precipitate preponderate asseverate

WORDLY WISE 26

AVOUCH, meaning "to assert positively," is falling out of current use in America and is being replaced by the phrase "vouch for."

DEBAUCHED means "morally corrupted"; do not confuse this word with the verb *debouch*, which means "to emerge from; to discharge" (soldiers debouching from a narrow pass; a bus debouching its passengers).

Be careful not to confuse any of these three terms: ENDEMIC, meaning "restricted to a particular area" (malaria is endemic to tropical countries); *epidemic* (Word List 17), the term given to the widespread occurrence of a disease (an epidemic of chicken pox); *pandemic* (Word List 23), meaning "occurring over a wide area; affecting many people." (Panic was pandemic. Malaria was pandemic throughout the entire region.) Note that *pandemic* can also be a noun and means "an epidemic of unusually large proportions."

WINSOME, meaning "winning," or "cheerful," is derived from the Old English *wynn* ("joy"). *Sum* was an Anglo-Saxon suffix used to form a new adjective from a noun or another adjective. Very few Old English words formed with *sum* are still in use, but the 14th century has given us these words from Middle English: *cumbersome, fulsome, handsome,* and *wholesome. Quarrelsome, adventuresome,* and *lonesome* date from the 16th century and later.

Etymology

Study the roots and prefixes given below together with the English words derived from them. Capitalized words are those given in the Word List. You should look up in a dictionary any words that are unfamiliar to you.

Prefixes: (review) *ante-* (before) Latin — Examples: *ANTE*DILUVIAN, *ante*rior, *ante*cedent
en- (in) Greek — Examples: *EN*DEMIC, *en*thusiast

Roots: *leva, levit* (lighten, raise) Latin — Examples: *LEVIT*ATION, *levity,* *eleva*tor
odein (sing) Greek — Examples: THREN*ODY, ode,* mel*ody*

Word List 27

ARGOSY	ELIDE	ORNITHOLOGY
CENTAUR	ENTITY	PROLETARIAT
COMPLIANT	GENTILITY	QUIXOTIC
DELIQUESCE	HERITAGE	STOICAL
DROSS	LISTLESS	VACUOUS

Look up the words above in your dictionary. Note that many of them have more than one meaning. When you feel that you know *all* the meanings of *all* the words, go on to the following exercises.

EXERCISE 27A

From the four choices following each phrase or sentence, you are to circle the letter preceding the one that is closest in meaning to the italicized word. Where the same word appears more than once, you should note that it is being used in different senses.

1. an *argosy* on the horizon (a) splendid ocean liner (b) heavily-laden merchant ship (c) well-armed ship of war (d) small tropical island

2. an *argosy* of good reading (a) grave scarcity (b) total neglect (c) gentle reminder (d) rich store

3. a picture of a *centaur* (a) creature half fish and half woman (b) creature half man and half horse (c) creature half goat and half man (d) creature half man and half bull

4. a *compliant* person (a) submissive (b) complicated (c) domineering (d) cunning

5. to *deliquesce* (a) worsen because of lack of restraint (b) express delight (c) bow or curtsy in an elaborate manner (d) become liquid through absorbing water

6. large amounts of *dross* (a) gold (b) money (c) impurities (d) information

7. to *elide* a passage (a) underline (b) read aloud (c) strike out (d) dictate

8. to *elide* a vowel (a) slur over (b) emphasize (c) write out (d) put an accent mark over

9. a complete *entity* (a) answer to an objection (b) figment of the imagination (c) thing that exists (d) lack of understanding

10. signs of *gentility* (a) weakness (b) strength (c) kindness (d) refinement

11. a proud *heritage* (a) aristocrat (b) nation (c) manner (d) tradition

12. to be *listless* (a) lacking in health (b) lacking in vigor (c) lacking in morality (d) lacking in money

13. an interest in *ornithology* (a) the study of birds (b) the study of reptiles (c) the study of fish (d) the study of insects

14. to represent the *proletariat* (a) writers and artists of a country (b) members of the aristocracy (c) members of the middle class (d) industrial working class

15. *quixotic* ideas (a) futuristic but attainable (b) workable but old-fashioned (c) idealistic but impractical (d) unfamiliar but adaptable

16. a *stoical* person (a) pleasure-seeking and pain-avoiding (b) indifferent to pain or pleasure (c) in almost constant pain (d) intensely argumentative

17. a *vacuous* stare (a) fixed (b) hostile (c) stupid (d) bold

18. *vacuous* space (a) limited (b) empty (c) vast (d) unlimited

Check your answers against the correct ones given below. The answers are not in order; this is to prevent your eye from catching sight of the correct answers before you have had a chance to do the exercise on your own.

13a. 2d. 12b. 1b. 16b. 9c. 3b. 14d. 17c. 11d. 5d. 7c. 18b. 4a. 6c. 15c. 8a. 10d.

Look up in your dictionary all the words for which you gave incorrect answers. Only when you have done this should you go on to the next exercise.

EXERCISE 27B

Each word in Word List 27 is used several times in the following sentences to illustrate different meanings or usage. One of the sentences for each word uses the italicized word incorrectly. You are to circle the letter preceding that sentence.

1. (a) "Stool pigeon" is thieves' *argosy* for a police informer. (b) The *argosy* was laden with spices from the East. (c) The book is an *argosy* of Indian folklore and legend. (d) The *argosy* of five merchant ships was a rich prize for the pirates.

2. (a) A *centaur* was a mythical beast with a man's head and trunk and a horse's body. (b) The *centaurs* were believed by the Greeks to dwell in the mountains of Thessaly. (c) A *centaur* was a Roman officer with command of one hundred foot-soldiers.

3. (a) He is extremely *compliant* and does whatever his friends suggest. (b) The rope should be very *compliant* so that it can be knotted easily. (c) She is willing to act in *compliance* with your wishes.

4. (a) They admitted their guilt and were sent to a home for *deliquescent* children. (b) These substances will *deliquesce* unless they are kept in moisture-free containers. (c) The moisture-laden air caused the *deliquescence* of the crystals.

5. (a) The metal is purified, and the *dross* that has been removed from it is discarded. (b) There is a great deal of *dross* in even the best of her plays. (c) The grain is beaten with flails to separate the wheat from the *dross*. (d) She was a true saint and regarded the riches of the world as mere *dross*.

6. (a) She *elided* certain passages that she thought might be misunderstood by her listeners. (b) The plane *elided* over the field, the pilot looking for a safe place to land. (c) Changes of pronunciation are brought about by the *eliding* of certain sounds. (d) "There is" become "There's" by a process of *elision*.

7. (a) Following the uniting of the various states, Italy became a political *entity*. (b) When we speak of postwar Germany, we are speaking of two separate *entities*. (c) We rejected the idea in its *entity* as it was completely worthless.

8. (a) The rough pioneers of the West cared nothing for the *gentility* of a person's background. (b) He handled the wounded animal with such *gentility* that it never once cried out. (c) Her air of *gentility* made men feel protective toward her. (d) The refined accents,

the airs of amused detachment, these were the hallmarks of *gentility*.

9. (a) The lakes and forests are part of our national *heritage* and must be protected. (b) We must guard what we have *heritaged* and pass it on to our descendents. (c) A sturdy independence is one of the precious *heritages* of our country.

10. (a) He had a *listless* telephone so that strangers could not annoy him by calling him up. (b) Her *listless* manner makes me think she is ill. (c) He greeted me *listlessly* and slumped back in his chair. (d) The heat had made everyone *listless*, and no one wanted to play tennis.

11. (a) She is particularly interested in the *ornithology* of sea birds. (b) The migration of birds is a subject falling within the province of *ornithology*. (c) J.J. Audubon, whose drawings of birds are world famous, was the father of *ornithology* in this country. (d) *Ornithologists* encourage bird-watching, as it greatly increases our store of knowledge.

12. (a) Karl Marx called upon the *proleteriat* to unite and throw off its chains. (b) A discontented *proletariat* provides a fertile breeding ground for the seeds of revolution. (c) He was a successful factory owner with two hundred *proletariats* working for him. (d) She was a woman of *proletarian* background who rose to a position of wealth and power.

13. (a) The town is located in one of the most *quixotic* islands of the Caribbean. (b) She presented a *quixotic* scheme that was supposed to make poverty a thing of the past. (c) He set out *quixotically* to right the wrongs of the world. (d) She has a *quixotic* imagniation, and no one takes her too seriously.

14. (a) The guerrillas were taught to remain *stoical* even under torture. (b) The wound was extremely *stoical*, yet he refused any treatment for it. (c) She was a *stoic*, indifferent

equally to pain and pleasure. (d) Despite her great pain, she attended *stoically* to her duties.

15. (a) She gave a *vacuous* grin when I asked her to explain her answer. (b) Interstellar space is not entirely *vacuous*; traces of galactic dust are everywhere. (c) The house has been *vacuous* for years because of rumors that it is haunted. (d) Say "I don't know" instead of using such *vacuous* expressions as "Search me."

EXERCISE 27C

This exercise combines synonyms and antonyms. You are to underline the word which is *either* most similar in meaning *or* most nearly opposite in meaning to the capitalized word. Underline only one word for each question after deciding that it is either an antonym or a synonym, and write A (for antonym) or S (for synonym) after the capitalized word. Allow 15 minutes only for this test. If you cannot answer a question, go on to the next without delay. If you have time left over at the end, go back and try to fill in unanswered questions.

26 or over correct:	excellent
22 to 25 correct:	good
21 or under correct:	thorough review of A exercises indicated

1. REFRACTORY . . . .
   endemic   analgesic   demulcent   compliant   grandiose

2. INTELLIGENT . . . .
   consummate vacuous frangible quixotic homogeneous

3. TOUGH . . . .
   fulgent precipitate frangible obtuse sterling

4. INTELLECTUAL . . . .
   grandiose chauvinist cerebral seismic evanescent

5. IMPURITIES . . . .
   attrition argosy dross contumely habiliments

107

6. MODERN . . . .
antediluvian risqué winsome nonpareil unimpeachable

7. PLEASED . . . .
demulcent aggrieved fustian diaphanous sapient

8. LIKENESS . . . .
attrition effigy dissonance threnody solecism

9. PRAISE . . . .
avouch contumely deliquesce elide mesmerize

10. SPEED . . . .
celerity dross levitation solecism vertigo

11. FEATHER . . . .
sachet centaur fakir queue quill

12. IMPROPER . . . .
endemic compliant risqué inalienable viviparous

13. SLUR . . . .
elide avouch dissonance cadence suffuse

14. DECLARE . . . .
imbue resurrect nominee avouch disdain

15. GARB . . . .
dishabille habiliments entity threnody marquetry

16. IRRITANT . . . .
demulcent epitome embrasure doctrine axiom

17. REALISTIC . . . .
vacuous cerebral quixotic listless subterranean

18. PLEASANT . . . .
vacuous sonic winsome contiguous hirsute

19. PIGTAIL . . . .
quizzical milliner quill dewlap queue

20. HYPNOTIZE . . . .
bedizen precipitate lionize exorcise mesmerize

21. MODEST . . . .
overweening cerebral compliant bereft halcyon

22. VIRTUOUS . . . .
stoical debauched analgesic verdant magniloquent

23. TRUTHFULNESS . . . .
aspersion gentility levitation mendacity zenith

24. RASH . . . .
effigy ersatz passé precipitate neuter

25. UNDERGROUND . . . .
rudimentary proletarian subterranean surrogate colloquial

26. HAPPY . . . .
antediluvian dolorous empyrean laconic equivocal

27. REFINEMENT . . . .
epitome contumely gentility heritage concomitant

28. REJOICE . . . .
deliquesce elide obviate inveigle repine

29. HARMONY . . . .
dross argosy effigy dissonance gentility

30. VIGOROUS . . . .
sebaceous winsome sonic viviparous listless

WORDLY WISE 27

The adjective form of *stoic* is either *stoic* or STOICAL (a stoic manner; a stoical attitude).

Etymology

Study the roots given below together with the English words derived from them. Capitalized words are those given in the Word List. You should look up in a dictionary any words that are unfamiliar to you.

Roots: *vacuus* (empty) Latin — Examples: *VAC*U*OUS, ev*acu*ate, *vacu*um
heres (heir) Latin — Examples: *HER*IT-AGE, in*her*it, *here*ditary

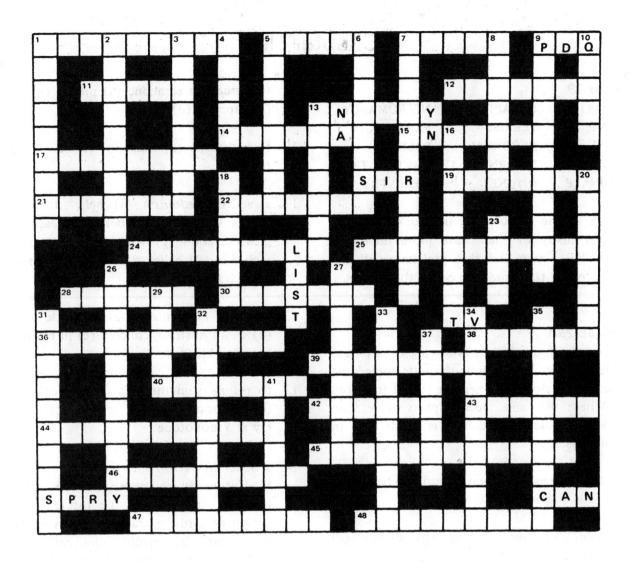

ACROSS

1. morally corrupted; depraved
5. a large feather used as a pen
7. of or relating to sound
11. a Muslim holy man
12. pleasantly cheerful
13. a thing that exists as a separate being
14. indifferent to pain or pleasure
15. an area enclosed by foreign territory
17. of or relating to the brain or intellect
19. sharply worded; biting (6)
21. a person named as a candidate
22. devoid of intelligence; stupid
24. insulting language or treatment
25. to cause to happen too soon
28. a whirlpool or tornado (19)
30. covered with hair; hairy (7)
36. the dress suited to a calling or occasion
38. a crudely made representation of a person
39. one who makes or sells women's hats
40. something that embodies an ideal
42. slightly improper; verging on the indecent
43. a richly laden ship or fleet of ships
44. that cannot be taken away
45. old-fashioned; antiquated
46. refinement or elegance of manner
47. pretentiously exaggerated
48. to induce a trance-like state; to hypnotize

DOWN

1. a substance that soothes inflamed tissue
2. a pain-killing drug
3. traditions; culture handed down from the past
4. impurities; worthless matter
5. romantically idealistic but impractical
6. lacking energy; languid
7. underground
8. a mythical creature, half man and half horse
9. the industrial working class
10. a tail-like braid of hair; a pigtail
13. the study of the relation between living things and their environment
16. submissive; yielding
18. to assert positively
20. a song of lamentation
23. an opening caused by splitting (24)
26. the study of birds
27. a gradual weakening or wearing down
29. to slur over; to omit
31. a fanatically patriotic person
32. the apparent raising of a body by supernatural means
33. to become liquid through absorbing moisture
34. the everyday language of common people (5)
35. lack of harmony or agreement
37. restricted or native to a particular area
41. a great musical artist (2)

Chapter Ten

Word List 28

AGGREGATE	ENRAPTURE	NECROMANCY
CLEMENT	FEBRILE	PARAPLEGIA
CONGEAL	HEDONISM	POLEMIC
DEFECT	INCARNATE	RAMIFICATIONS
DISSEMINATE	INTONE	SOPHISTRY

Look up the words above in your dictionary. Note that many of them have more than one meaning. When you feel that you know *all* the meanings of *all* the words, go on to the exercises below.

EXERCISE 28A

From the four choices following each phrase or sentence, you are to circle the letter preceding the one that is closest in meaning to the italicized word. Where the same word appears more than once, you should note that it is being used in different senses.

1. in the *aggregate* (a) total amount (b) beginning (c) final stages (d) secluded area

2. *clement* weather (a) wet (b) stormy (c) changeable (d) mild

3. a plea for *clemency* (a) peace (b) justice (c) mercy (d) honesty

4. to *congeal* in cold weather (a) shiver (b) thicken (c) sleep (d) turn white

5. to quickly *congeal* (a) hide (b) become liquid (c) agree (d) become solid

6. a serious *defect* (a) matter (b) omission (c) fault (d) talk

7. to *defect* to the enemy (a) return (b) switch sides (c) point (d) turn one's back

8. to *disseminate* knowledge (a) distort (b) suppress (c) spread (d) worship

9. to *enrapture* someone (a) pursue (b) punish (c) imprison (d) delight

10. to be *febrile* (a) weak (b) feverish (c) gentle (d) cold

11. a selfish *hedonism* (a) belief that charity begins at home (b) belief that pleasure is the greatest good (c) withdrawal into a life of seclusion (d) belief that God will provide for one's wants

12. the devil *incarnate* (a) as the cause of all evil (b) as an abstract concept (c) in bodily form (d) in all his forms

13. to *intone* something (a) say absentmindedly (b) say soothingly (c) say threateningly (d) say in a monotone

14. a belief in *necromancy* (a) the foretelling of the future by communication with the dead (b) the foretelling of the future by examination of birds' entrails (c) the foretelling of the future by reading the cards (d) the foretelling of the future by examination of a person's palm

15. suffering from *paraplegia* (a) inflammation of the joints (b) a gradual deterioration of the brain (c) a fusing of the spinal bones (d) paralysis of the lower part of the body

16. engaged in *polemics* (a) water sports (b) gymnastics (c) deep discussions (d) disputes

17. many *ramifications* (a) defense installations (b) far-reaching consequences (c) physical assaults (d) whispered rumors

18. an example of *sophistry* (a) the art of fine penmanship (b) unintentional humor (c) a strict adherence to the truth (d) clever but misleading reasoning

Check your answers against the correct ones given below. The answers are not in order; this is to prevent your eye from catching sight of the correct answers before you have had a chance to do the exercise on your own.

8c. 3c. 15d. 17b. 14a. 13d. 2d. 11b. 6c. 5d. 4b. 1a. 12c. 10b. 18d. 16d. 9d. 7b.

Look up in your dictionary all the words for which you gave incorrect answers. Only when you have done this should you go on to the next exercise.

EXERCISE 28B

Each word in Word List 28 is used several times in the sentences below to illustrate different meanings or usage. One of the sentences for each word uses the italicized word incorrectly. You are to circle the letter preceding that sentence.

1. (a) The *aggregate* of human knowledge increased greatly during this period. (b) New York contains the greatest *aggregation* of buildings in the world. (c) Scratching that sore place will only *aggregate* it. (d) People left the country and *aggregated* in the towns and cities.

2. (a) The judge dealt *clemently* with the convicted thief and gave him a light sentence. (b) Birds leave the northern regions for the more *clement* climes of the south. (c) We plan to go boating tomorrow if the present *clement* weather continues. (d) She tried to *clement* friendly relations between the two groups but with small success.

3. (a) She felt her blood *congeal* as she thought of the ordeal facing her. (b) A rather *congeal* greeting awaited them at the hotel. (c) The low temperature has caused the oil in the crankcase to *congeal*. (d) The somewhat fluid class divisions of the early Middle Ages *congealed* into the feudal system of the later medieval period.

4. (a) There is a *defect* in the steering assembly that could cause a bad accident. (b) A child with a contagious disease should be isolated lest he *defect* other children. (c) The five sailors who *defected* to the West last month gave a press conference today. (d) The *defective* eyesight of these people is probably caused by vitamin deficiencies.

5. (a) The main purpose of missionary work is to *disseminate* God's word. (b) Thomas Huxley saw to it that Darwin's ideas on evolution were widely *disseminated*. (c) Silt from the river is *disseminated* over a wide area. (d) She *disseminated*, refusing either to admit or deny her guilt.

6. (a) We were *enraptured* by the beauty and grace of her performance. (b) He gazed *enraptured* into the eyes of the woman he loved. (c) Oh, to be in love and filled with that first fine, careless *enrapture*!

7. (a) The book deals humorously with the *febrile* pitch of activity that precedes a Broadway opening night. (b) His *febrile* condition is the result of a malarial infection contracted years before. (c) Her muscles had grown *febrile* from lack of use and were quite wasted away.

8. (a) Most of us find a view of life somewhere between the extremes of asceticism and *hedonism*. (b) *Hedonists* believe that pleasure or happiness is the sole or chief good in life. (c) They are very tolerant parents and overlook a number of their children's *hedonisms*. (d) She claims that a *hedonistic* philosophy is not necessarily an irresponsible one.

9. (a) He is purity and goodness *incarnate*. (b) The priest's muttered *incarnations* were supposed to have magical properties. (c) In the Christian faith, the *Incarnation* is the assumption of bodily form by Christ. (d) The Japanese emperor was regarded as a god *incarnate*.

10. (a) The watchman *intoned* the hours of the night as he made his rounds. (b) The priest

intoned the words of the burial service in a high, nasal voice. (c) Your *intonation* that I took the money is strongly resented. (d) We can tell the difference between a statement and a question by the *intonation* of the voice.

11. (a) *Necromancy*, the foretelling of the future by communicating with the dead, is a form of black magic. (b) Having to go through the churchyard after dark made us feel very *necromantic*. (c) This book on black magic contains many *necromantic* spells. (d) The natives were terrified of the witch doctor's powers as a *necromancer*.

12. (a) Doctors operated for over four hours to remove a *paraplegia* from the patient's spine. (b) The soldier suffering from *paraplegia* told us he had been hit in the spine with a piece of shrapnel. (c) *Paraplegics*, although confined to wheelchairs, are able to lead relatively normal lives. (d) An entire ward of the hospital is given over to *paraplegic* patients.

13. (a) She wore a *polemic* around her neck to ward off evil spirits. (b) The discussion grew *polemic* and had to be ended abruptly. (b) He is a confirmed *polemicist,* never happier than when disputing with someone. (d) Let us keep the discussion on a high level and not descend to *polemics.*

14. (a) We have not yet explored all the *ramifications* of this new theory. (b) She brooded on the *ramifications* of what she had heard. (c) A system of *ramifications* had been set up to defend the town from attack.

15. (a) Her reasoning, seemingly plausible but actually misleading, is pure *sophistry*. (b) The *Sophists* were a Greek sect who were able to prove anything by logic. (c) The *sophistry* of his arguments will mislead only the very young and the very naive. (d) There was a hint of *sophistry* in her smile as she greeted me.

EXERCISE 28C

Describe the origin of, and the story behind, the following words:

SYBARITE (Word List 13) . . . .

. . . .

. . . .

CHAUVINIST (Word List 26) . . . .

. . . .

MESMERIZE (Word List 25) . . . .

. . . .

. . . .

QUIXOTIC (Word List 27) . . . .

. . . .

. . . .

. . . .

WORDLY WISE 28

The adjective POLEMIC, meaning "of or involving dispute," may also be written *polemical* (a polemical writer; polemic articles).

In the singular, the noun POLEMIC means "an attack on the principles or opinions of another" (he wrote a polemic instead of a review); the plural is usually used to refer to the art or practice of controversy (his style of argument rarely rises above polemics).

The Sophists of Greece professed to be able to make men wise (*sophos*), but their rhetoric was often better than their reasoning. The complexity of their arguments made them persuasive and seemingly plausible, but Socrates accused the Sophists of using false logic "to make the lesser thing appear the greater" and a bad thing seem good. Thus SOPHISTRY is a pejorative term applied to specious or deceptive reasoning. The same pejorative sense conditions the meaning of *sophomoric*, meaning "conceited and overconfident of having knowledge, but poorly informed and immature." *Sophisticate* originally meant "to deal with in an artificial way, to deprive of simplicity, to mislead or falsify"; it has acquired more favorable meanings, however, and has come to describe something complex, subtle, worldly-wise or intellectually appealing (a sophisticated machine; a sophisticated New Yorker; a sophisticated novel). *Sophistical* is now the adjective to use to suggest the deceptive argumentation characteristic of sophistry.

Etymology

Study the roots given below together with the English words derived from them. Capitalized words are those given in the Word List. You should look up in a dictionary any words unfamiliar to you.

Roots: *carnis* (flesh) Latin — Examples: IN-CARNATE, *carn*ivorous, *carn*al

necros (corpse) Greek — Examples: NECROMANCY, *necro*polis

Word List 29

AMITY	FRIABLE	OBLIQUITY
COHORT	HIBERNATE	PATRICIAN
CONTINGENT	INGOT	RABID
DESECRATE	LAUDATORY	RAPPORT
DISTRAIT	MOBILIZE	SUPPOSITION
EPICURE		

Look up the above words in your dictionary. Note that many of them have more than one meaning. When you feel that you know *all* the meanings of *all* the words, go on to the following exercises.

EXERCISE 29A

From the four choices following each phrase or sentence, you are to circle the letter preceding the one that is closest in meaning to the italicized word. Where the same word appears more than once, you should note that it is being used in different senses.

1. lasting *amity* (a) bitterness (b) friendship (c) suspicion (d) contempt

2. a Roman *cohort* (a) company of soldiers (b) head of the Senate (c) armed sailing ship (d) award of honor

3. a *cohort* of someone (a) enemy (b) critic (c) superior (d) follower

4. a large *contingent* (a) list of persons eligible to vote (b) group comprising part of a larger group (c) claim unsupported by evidence (d) sum of money drawing interest

5. *contingent* upon (a) drawing (b) touching (c) balanced (d) conditional

6. any *contingency* (a) reason (b) possibility (c) excuse (d) amount

7. to *desecrate* a church (a) violate the sacredness of (b) set apart for religious purposes (c) cease to use for religious purposes (d) uphold the sacredness of

8. to be *distrait* (a) attentive (b) calm (c) inattentive (d) suspicious

9. He is an *epicure*. (a) person who practices self-denial (b) person with highly-cultivated tastes (c) person practicing medicine without a license (d) person who takes a pessimistic view of life

10. a *friable* substance (a) easily-crumbled (b) formed of crystals (c) edible (d) poisonous

11. to *hibernate* (a) travel widely searching for food (b) sleep during the winter (c) store food away for the winter (d) change one's coloration during the winter

12. a gold *ingot* (a) coin (b) medallion (c) thread (d) bar

13. *laudatory* words (a) expressing optimism (b) expressing shame (c) expressing praise (d) expressing displeasure

14. to *mobilize* (a) change one's mind frequently (b) move freely (c) prepare for a state of war (d) be frozen with fear

15. to cover up one's *obliquity* (a) departure from what is right (b) superior knowledge (c) grief at someone's death (d) feeling of shame

16. a series of *obliquities* (a) indivisible numbers (b) confusing statements (c) explanatory diagrams (d) major disasters

17. *patrician* tastes (a) uncultivated (b) broad (c) exotic (d) aristocratic

18. a dog that is *rabid* (a) able to track animals (b) vicious by nature (c) affectionate by nature (d) dangerously diseased

19. a *rabid* follower (a) disloyal (b) fanatical (c) faithful (d) unwilling

20. She became *rabid.* (a) rather nervous (b) very weary (c) completely bewildered (d) extremely violent

21. to achieve *rapport* (a) understanding of oneself (b) one's ultimate ambition (c) a sympathetic relationship with others (d) a state of perfect peace of mind

22. a mere *supposition* (a) person in a subordinate position (b) offer to help that promises little (c) assumption that something is true (d) belief that flies in the face of the facts

Check your answers against the correct ones given below. The answers are not in order; this is to prevent your eye from catching sight of the correct answers before you have had a chance to do the exercise on your own.

8c. 3d. 14c. 17d. 21c. 15a. 13c. 2a. 11b. 6b. 19b. 20d. 5d. 22c. 4b. 1b. 12d. 10a. 18d. 16b. 9b. 7a.

Look up in your dictionary all the words for which you gave incorrect answers. Only when you have done this should you go on to the next exercise.

EXERCISE 29B

Each word in Word List 29 is used several times in the sentences below to illustrate different meanings or usage. One of the sentences for each word uses the italicized word incorrectly. You are to circle the letter preceding that sentence.

1. (a) Only where there is *amity* between nations can there be world peace. (b) There was a bitter rivalry between the two groups although they kept up a pretence of *amity*. (c) Britain and France were once enemies but are now *amities.*

2. (a) A Roman legion consisted of ten *cohorts*, each with 300 to 600 men. (b) She praised them for doing well but *cohorted* them to do even better in the future. (c) The outlaw chief and a few of his *cohorts* tried to take over the little town. (d) She denied being one of the mayor's *cohorts* and said she scarcely knew the mayor.

3. (a) A fresh *contingent* of troops joined the army just prior to the battle. (b) A reserve fund was set up to meet any *contingencies* that might arise. (c) Success is *contingent* on our getting there first. (d) She has a large *contingent* of money put away for when she needs it.

4. (a) They *desecrated* the Bible by tearing out some of the pages to make paper darts. (b) The priest grieved over the *desecration* of his church when the enemy soldiers used it as a barracks. (c) The entire village was *desecrated* by the fire that swept through it. (c) You *desecrate* the memory of your dear grandfather by saying such things about him.

5. (a) She seemed *distrait* for some reason and was quite unable to concentrate on her work. (b) These children become *distrait* very quickly and it is difficult to recapture their attention.

114

(c) A deep loyalty to their masters is one of the *distraits* of cocker spaniels. (d) They were often *distrait* during their son's illness, and scarcely seemed to hear my questions.

6. (a) The food in this hotel is an *epicure*'s delight. (b) Peach melba is a dessert first *epicured* for the famed opera star Nellie Melba. (c) He is an *epicure* and savors to the fullest the delights of the table. (d) The meal was a memorable one with an assortment of *epicurean* dishes.

7. (a) He looked a most *friable* figure as he stood there with tears in his eyes. (b) Sandstone is much more *friable* than a hard rock such as granite. (c) Fresh bread is not as *friable* as bread that is slightly stale.

8. (a) Certain mammals *hibernate* during the winter months when food is in short supply. (b) Bears emerge from *hibernation* on the first warm day in spring. (c) The former president emerged from political *hibernation* today with his first public appearance in more than a year. (d) Squirrels *hibernate* nuts during the fall so that they will have food for winter.

9. (a) Metal is cast into *ingots* of a suitable size for transportation. (b) Each *ingot* is stamped with its weight and degree of purity of the metal. (c) There are large *ingot* deposits in northern Labrador waiting to be tapped.

10. (a) Your *laudatory* remarks were appreciated, but I don't feel I deserved such praise. (b) They made a *laudatory* attempt to save the drowning man but were, alas, unsuccessful. (c) She made a *laudatory* speech commending us all for our efforts.

11. (a) She *mobilized* the car by jamming the steering mechanism. (b) The entire country quickly *mobilized* for war when peace talks were broken off. (c) Soldiers returned to civilian life after military service are said to have been *demobilized*. (d) The dimensions of this disaster require the prompt *mobilization* of all our resources.

12. (a) She admits her *obliquity* and promises to do better in the future. (b) The *obliquity* of the material makes it completely lightproof. (c) He hid true intentions behind a smoke screen of *obliquities*.

13. (a) She was a renowned *patrician* of the arts, donating millions to music and the theatre. (b) In the early days of Rome, the *patricians* ruled over the plebeians. (c) Rulers have traditionally been drawn from the *patrician* class, and our own country is no exception. (d) His air of *patrician* elegance was intended to impress those of more humble birth.

14. A *rabid* dog can transmit rabies, a disease causing choking and convulsions in humans. (b) She became *rabid* at the thought that her friend had been deceiving her. (c) She used to be a *rabid* fan of the old Brooklyn Dodgers. (d) The *rabidity* with which he completed the task astonished us all.

15. (a) There was a fine *rapport* between the singer and her accompanist. (b) He had a distinct *rapport* of uneasiness, as though something terrible were about to befall him. (c) The painter found it hard to achieve a *rapport* with her subject.

16. (a) The *supposition* that all human beings are equal is one that I would challenge. (b) Your statement that the method will work is pure *supposition*, as it has not yet been tested. (c) He was very *suppositions* and would never walk under a ladder.

EXERCISE 29C

Complete the following analogies by underlining the numbered pair of words which are related to each other in the same way as the first pair are related.

1. cardiac:heart:: (1) weak:stomach (2) cerebral: intelligent (3) vein:blood (4) cerebral:brain (5) intelligence:brain

2. ordinal:second:: (1) cardinal:third (2) three: third (3) cardinal:two (4) second:two (5) second:third

3. patrician:plebeian:: (1) Roman:Greek (2) town: country (3) ancient:modern (4) aristocrat: commoner (5) peace:war

4. self-indulgence:self-denial:: (1) chauvinism: hedonism (2) sophistry:hedonism (3) chauvinism:marquetry (4) hedonism:asceticism (5) marquetry:asceticism

5. lionize:celebrity:: (1) deify:god (2) prognosticate:future (3) relate:story (4) bedizen:clothes (5) realize:ambition

6. ambulatory:walk: (1) immobile:stationary (2) start:stop (3) motion:propel (4) mobilize:war (5) mobile:move

7. impeccable:sullied:: (1) supposition:proof (2) grandiose:magniloquent (3) impecunious: wealthy (4) precipitate:hasty (5) tariff:import

8. patriotic:chauvinistic:: (1) loyal:disloyal (2) king:country (3) kingdom:republic (4) American:foreign (5) enthusiastic:rabid

WORDLY WISE 29

DISTRAIT (pronounced *di-STRAY*) means "inattentive; absentminded." *Distraught* (pronounced *di-STRAWT*) means "driven mad; crazed" (distraught with grief). *Distrait* is sometimes used to mean *distraught*, but it is better to keep the distinction between the two terms.

LAUDATORY means "expressing praise" (laudatory speeches); *laudable* means "worthy of praise" (a laudable attempt). These two terms should not be confused with each other.

Etymology

Study the following roots together with the English words derived from them. Capitalized words are those given in the Word List. You should look up in a dictionary any words that are unfamiliar to you.

Roots: *sacer* (holy) Latin — Examples: DE*SECR*ATE, *sacr*ilege, con*secr*ate
movere (move) Latin — Examples: *MOVI*LIZE, auto*mobi*le

Word List 30

AUTOCRAT	HANSOM	OBSIDIAN
COMMISERATE	IDIOSYNCRASY	PATRONIZE
DEFEATIST	INFILTRATE	RAFFISH
DISQUISITION	METAMORPHOSIS	RETRACT
EFFICACY	MONOTHEISM	TOREADOR
EXCERPT		

Look up the words above in your dictionary. Note that many of them have more than one meaning. When you feel that you know *all* the meanings of *all* the words, go on to the exercises below.

EXERCISE 30A

From the four choices following each phrase or sentence, you are to circle the letter preceding the one that is closest in meaning to the italicized word. Where the same word appears more than once, you should note that it is being used in different senses.

1. rule by an *autocrat* (a) monarch with no real power (b) monarch with unlimited power (c) member of a ruling group (d) representative of the people

2. to *commiserate* with someone (a) quarrel (b) debate (c) share happiness (d) sympathize

3. to be a *defeatist* (a) person lacking the will to win (b) person who turns defeat into victory (c) person determined to avoid defeat (d) person who learns from his defeats

4. a lengthy *disquisition* (a) scolding (b) argument (c) interrogation (d) discourse

5. the *efficacy* of something (a) purpose (b) origin (c) effectiveness (d) termination

6. a brief *excerpt* (a) interlude (b) explanation (c) rejoinder (d) extract

7. to get into a *hansom* (a) two-wheeled carriage (b) boat propelled by a pole (c) mood that one cannot shake off (d) interminable argument

8. a little *idiosyncrasy* (a) scenic route (b) diacritical mark over a letter (c) personal mannerism (d) dose of a narcotic drug

9. to *infiltrate* the enemy positions (a) blow up (b) pass through (c) observe (d) launch a frontal attack on

10. a complete *metamorphosis* (a) life history (b) state of collapse (c) change of form (d) range of sounds

11. the origins of *monotheism* (a) the belief that monarchs rule by consent of the governed (b) the belief that God and nature are one (c) the belief that all people have certain inalienable rights (d) the belief that there is only one God

12. to study the *obsidian* (a) giant lizardlike creature (b) glasslike volcanic rock (c) position of the sun at noon (d) deepest part of the ocean

13. to *patronize* a store (a) refuse to do business with (b) own jointly (c) persuade people to stay away from (d) shop regularly at

14. to *patronize* someone (a) go into partnership with (b) cut off relations with (c) act condescendingly toward (d) visit regularly

15. a *raffish* person (a) of stunted growth (b) somewhat disreputable (c) enormously fat (d) very absentminded

16. to *retract* a statement (a) issue (b) withdraw (c) compose (d) correct

17. a famous *toreador* (a) big game hunter (b) deep-sea fisherman (c) racing driver (d) bullfighter

Check your answers against the correct ones given above. The answers are not in order; this is to prevent your eye from catching sight of the correct answers before you have had a chance to do the exercise on your own.

9b. 12b. 2d. 14c. 17d. 11d. 5c. 10c. 7a. 4d. 6d. 15b. 8c. 3a. 13d. 1b. 16b.

Look up in your dictionary all the words for which you gave incorrect answers. Only when you have done this should you go on to the next exercise.

EXERCISE 30B

Each word in Word List 30 is used several times in the sentences below to illustrate different meanings or usage. One of the sentences for each word uses the italicized word incorrectly. You are to circle the letter preceding that sentence.

1. (a) Before the Revolution, Russia was an *autocracy* with the czar wielding unlimited power. (b) The head of the household in those days was a complete *autocrat* whose word was law. (c) King George's *autocratic* handling of his colonies led to the American Revolution. (d) On the queen's death, her eldest child succeeded to the throne *autocratically*.

2. (a) It's true that she expressed regret, but her *commiseration* seemed a little forced. (b) He *commiserated* with the widow in her tragic loss. (c) You will be given a job *commiserate* with your abilities.

3. (a) After the battle, victors and *defeatists* united to bury the dead. (b) Let us have no more of this *defeatist* talk while there is still a chance of victory. (c) A mood of *defeatism* swept the nation and prepared the way for its collapse. (d) Ignore the *defeatists* among you who say it is useless to continue the struggle.

4. (a) I'm afraid very few people in the audience understood the professor's *disquisition*. (b) I am writing a *disquisition* setting forth my ideas in detail. (c) The *disquisition* of the prisoner was conducted by police officers working in relays.

117

5. (a) The *efficacy* of aspirin in relieving headaches is well known. (b) Just how *efficacious* the United Nations can be in preventing war remains to be seen. (c) She is a firm believer in the *efficacy* of prayer. (d) The new law becomes *efficacious* on January 1 of next year.

6. (a) She has promised to read us a few *excerpts* from her recent book. (b) The record consists of *excerpts* from half a dozen popular operas. (c) Why should she *excerpt* herself from the rules that are binding on everyone else? (d) They *excerpted* these passages from books published in the last few years.

7. (a) It was a beautiful house, and they must have paid a *hansom* price for it. (b) The young couple climbed into the *hansom*, the driver cracked his whip, and they were on their way. (c) The *hansom*, a popular form of transportation in the late 19th century, was invented by Joseph Aloysius Hansom.

8. (a) We all have our little *idiosyncrasies*, and his is wearing his hat around the house. (b) They exchanged *idiosyncrasies* about the weather when they met each morning. (c) Their behavior became markedly *idiosyncratic*, and everyone thought them most peculiar.

9. (a) It was claimed that a number of communists had *infiltrated* the labor movement. (b) He succeeded in *infiltrating* two dollars out of me with his tale of woe. (c) Singly and in small groups, our troops *infiltrated* the enemy lines. (d) The *infiltration* of water through sand purefies it for drinking.

10. (a) The *metamorphosis* of the caterpillar into the butterfly is one of nature's marvels. (b) She decided that she needed a complete *metamorphosis* and went off for a week of fishing and swimming. (c) Homer's **Odyssey** tells of men being *metamorphosed* into swine. (d) The *metamorphosis* of wood into coal takes millions of years to accomplish.

11. (a) The Jews were the first people to adopt *monotheism* as their religion. (b) Moses was the first *monotheist* of whom we have a fully-documented account. (c) To a people worshiping many gods, the idea of *monotheism* must have seemed strange. (d) The priest intoned the prayers *monotheistically* as he lit the altar candles.

12. (a) The bones of huge *obsidians* that roamed the earth millions of years ago have been discovered as fossil remains. (b) *Obsidian* is an extremely hard, glasslike rock formed from the lava of volcanoes.

13. (a) She adopted a very *patronizing* attitude toward me which I strongly resented. (b) Areas where the crime rate is high are *patronized* by police officers at frequent intervals. (c) I have *patronized* this restaurant for years because of the excellent food it offers.

14. (a) She fell in with a group of *raffish* young people who exerted a bad influence on her. (b) The club he took me to was actually a gambling den in the most *raffish* part of town. (c) These people she calls her friends are nothing but *raffish*, and they will lead her into serious trouble. (d) The actor's good looks and *raffish* manner made him irresistible to his fans.

15. (a) That statement is untrue, and I demand that you *retract* it immediately. (b) The tortoise *retracts* its head into its shell when it is in danger. (c) Large aircraft have *retractable* landing gear for a more streamlined shape. (d) You can *retract* the money you lent me whenever it pleases you.

16. (a) A *toreador* must risk being gored by the bulls many times in the course of his career. (b) The bullfighter plunged his *toreador* into the bull's heart.

EXERCISE 30C

This exercise combines synonyms and antonyms. You are to underline the word which is *either* most similar in meaning *or* most nearly opposite in meaning to the capitalized word. Underline only one word for each question after deciding that it is either an antonym or a synonym, and write A (for antonym) or S (for synonym) after the capitalized word. Allow 15 minutes only for this test. If you cannot answer a question, go on to the next without delay. If you have time left over at the end, go back and try to fill in unanswered questions.

26 or over correct: excellent
22 to 25 correct: good
21 or under correct: thorough review of A
                        exercises indicated

1. ATTENTIVE . . . .
   cognate distrait concomitant bereft mordant

2. ASCETICISM . . . .
   malapropism chauvinism monotheism hedonism cornucopia

3. SYMPATHIZE . . . .
   commiserate intercede inveigle exculpate defray

4. HARSH . . . .
   ductile inviolate surrogate circumspect clement

5. RECTITUDE . . . .
   obliquity panacea disdain antipathy itinerary

6. COHERENT . . . .
   clairvoyant phlegmatic maudlin disjointed refractory

7. SPREAD . . . .
   prognosticate expiate disseminate masticate resurrect

8. ISSUE . . . .
   innuendo disdain retract emote ensemble

9. DISCOURSE . . . .
   axiom disquisition negotiate rostrum protocol

10. ENMITY . . . .
    option doctrine mendacity amity turpitude

11. ARISTOCRATIC . . . .
    surrogate acolyte dolorous potentate patrician

12. SCATTER . . . .
    leaven aggregate propound eviscerate educe

13. FANATICAL . . . .
    blasphemous climacteric rabid halcyon anomalous

14. IMPROVE . . . .
    exacerbate asseverate preponderate coalesce foment

15. FEVERISH . . . .
    febrile nugatory fulgent ambulatory fustian

16. CONSECRATE . . . .
    extradite reciprocate accouter accolade desecrate

17. USEFULNESS . . . .
    refutation jurisdiction efficacy atavism tribulation

18. SOLIDIFY . . . .
    expatiate correlate lave congeal elide

19. DELIGHT . . . .
    bedizen enrapture obviate paregoric solecism

20. SHUN . . . .
    repine patronize cuckold meander parole

21. FOLLOWER . . . .
    cohort pantheon apothecary phalanx sachet

22. NADIR . . . .
    initial leviathan sybarite firmament zenith

23. WEALTHY . . . .
    verdant sterling sapient impecunious hirsute

24. EXTRACT . . . .
    anoint excerpt objurgate pulsate dissemble

25. FAULT . . . .

blandishment depredation defect moratorium motif

26. ABUNDANT . . . .

baneful banal equivocal outmoded exiguous

27. CONDEMNATORY . . . .

gratuitous ethereal trajectory laudatory disconsolate

28. CONDITIONAL . . . .

panegyric homogeneous didactic precipitate contingent

29. MANNERISM . . . .

idiosyncrasy boon carapace vernacular panegyric

30. SOLID . . . .

lacteal beatific ethereal specious tactile

WORDLY WISE 30

EFFICACY is a noun meaning "effectiveness; usefulness." Four adjectives related to this word may cause confusion. *Effective* means "having the power to produce a desired result"; it also means "in effect" (to take effective measures; a law becoming effective on a certain date). *Effectual* means "doing what was hoped or intended." (Measures become effective when signed into law; only time will show whether or not they will be effectual.) *Efficient* means "producing the desired effect in the most economical way" (large estates are more efficient than small farms). *Efficacious* suggests the capability to achieve certain results when actually employed (stannous fluoride is an efficacious preventive of tooth decay, and putting it in the water supply is the most efficient way of dispensing it).

Toreador comes from the Spanish word *toro* (bull) and is the general term for a bullfighter. Bullfighting, a controversial sport, has been banned in some parts of Spain.

Etymology

Study the roots given below together with the English words derived from them. Capitalized words are those given in the Word List. You should look up in a dictionary any words that are unfamiliar to you.

Roots: *autos* (self) Greek – Examples: *AUTO-CRAT*, *auto*mobile, *auto*graph

kratos (power) Greek – Examples: AUTO-*CRAT*, demo*crat*, techno*crat*

mono (one) Greek – Examples: *MONO-THEISM*, *mono*poly, *mono*gamous

(review) *theos* (God) Greek – Examples: MONO*THE*ism, a*the*ism, pan*theon*

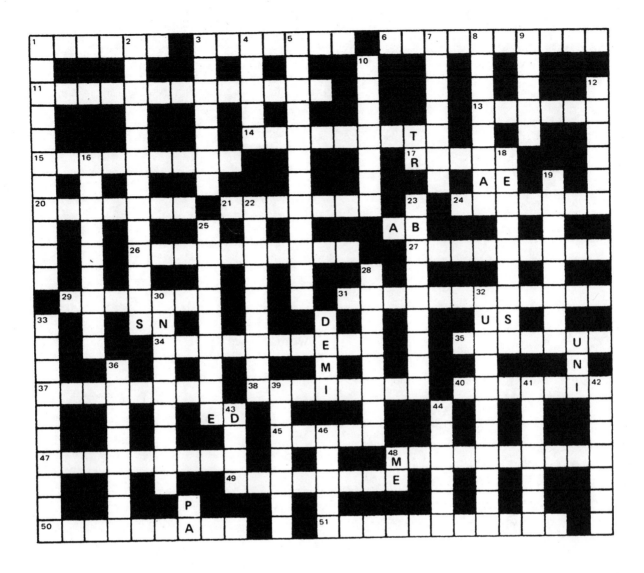

ACROSS

1. a follower or accomplice
3. slightly vulgar or disreputable
6. supposed foretelling of the future by communication with the dead
11. a marked or an abrupt change in form
13. to recite in a monotonous voice
14. to violate the sacredness of
15. clever but misleading reasoning
17. extremely violent
20. to take back or withdraw
21. a person with cultivated tastes
24. to change the pitch of the voice (5)
26. to pass through or into
27. expressing praise; commendatory
29. to treat or regard as a celebrity (13)
31. a learned speech or article; a discourse
34. depending on something unknown; conditional
35. the condition or amount most favorable (4)
37. a ruler with unlimited power
38. effectiveness; usefulness
40. of or involving dispute
45. metal in the shape of a bar
47. to fill with delight
48. the belief that there is only one God
49. to organize and make ready, as for war
50. a total or whole; a mass gathered together
51. to spread widely

DOWN

1. to feel or show pity or sympathy for
2. far-reaching consequences
3. a sympathetic relationship between people
4. a narrow inlet of the sea (20)
5. a personal mannerism; a quirk
7. to thicken and become solid
8. glasslike volcanic rock
9. friendly, peaceful relations
10. feverish; fevered
12. to desert one's country for another
16. of noble birth; aristocratic
18. lacking the will to win
19. the belief that pleasure is the greatest good
22. to favor in a condescending way
23. departure from what is right
25. to spend the winter in a sleeplike state
28. absentminded; inattentive
30. given bodily form
32. something assumed to be true
33. paralysis of the lower part of the body
36. a bullfighter
39. easily crumbled
41. a passage selected or quoted; an extract
42. merciful; lenient
43. to consider; to believe (15)
44. a two-wheeled, horse-drawn carriage
46. extremely cold; icy (19)